Historical Reason

by JOSÉ ORTEGA Y GASSET

JOSÉ ORTEGA Y GASSET

HISTORICAL
REASON

TRANSLATED BY PHILIP W. SILVER

W · W · NORTON & COMPANY
New York   London

The text of this book is composed in Janson, with display type set in Futura
Medium. Composition by Vail-Ballou Press, Inc. Manufacturing by The
Murray Printing Company.

First Edition

Library of Congress Cataloging in Publication Data

Ortega y Gasset, José, 1883–1955.
   Historical reason.

   Translation of: Sobre la razón histórica.
   1. Rationalism.   I. Title.
B4568.O73S6213   1983   196'.1   83-13139

ISBN 0-393-01831-8

W. W. Norton & Company, Inc.
500 Fifth Avenue, New York, N.Y. 10110
W. W. Norton & Company Ltd.
37 Great Russell Street, London WC1B 3NU

1 2 3 4 5 6 7 8 9 0

Contents

Translator's Note

AS THE EDITOR, Paulino Garagorri, points out, the text here translated was essentially a transcription of two cycles of lectures that Ortega gave. Clearly they were delivered, as was his custom, from notes based on the intricate filing system that he used. Thus the resulting text was the record of an oral, extempore presentation from scant notes, with one or two passages read from printed or written works.

So as to preserve the viva voce effect of the original, I have used a rather informal style in the translation. But to maintain the spontaneity of the Spanish, I have also had to clip Ortega's wings a bit and condense some of his long, rolling periods. Otherwise the tone of the whole would have missed the mark of what Ortega and his translator wished to set before his English reader.

Philip W. Silver

Introduction

IN SEPTEMBER and October of 1940, in the Faculty of Philosophy and Letters of the University of Buenos Aires, Ortega gave a course consisting of five lectures with the title "Historical Reason." Subsequently, in November and December of 1944, in the Faculty of Letters of the University of Lisbon, he gave another course with the same title—discontinued, it also amounted to only five lectures. With the present volume, which contains the texts of both courses and appears under their common title, we again take up the project of making available Ortega's unpublished works.

What the reader is offered here comes from two sources: one is the manuscript notes Ortega wrote prior to his lectures; the other is the stenographic copy that seems to have been taken at the time of the actual lectures. This edition follows the oral version, but the manuscript notes have been useful in clarifying, ordering, or completing various passages. All additions to the author's words are enclosed in brackets.

Even though both courses have the same title, they contain quite different specific developments, which may have been part of the projected work that Ortega announced repeatedly as "The Dawn of Historical Reason." The following pages, then, are a singularly important part of his philosophical legacy.

As everyone knows, today the concept of philosophy—like all else, without exception—is in a state of crisis, and the meaning of the term itself is particularly confusing. Under the name—either explicit or oblique—of philosophy, the most diverse products are offered, in which it is often unclear what the writer intends or what point is being addressed. For this reason the reader—the reader, that is, who has still not given up, who has yet to lose "the appetite for knowledge" (which characterizes "all mankind," as Aristotle, the optimist, stated at the beginning of his *Metaphysics*)—will do well to begin this posthumous work by Ortega with some foreknowledge of the matter.

The subject, as I understand it, is that the fate of Western man and the world he has built was conditioned to a great extent by the kind of thinking practiced by the philosophers of ancient Greece. For man uses thought, consciously or not, according to preconceived ideas about his intellectual apparatus. During the historical course of human thought, crises and transformations have brought human life in its long—or, if you prefer, brief—span to the exceptionally profound crisis that obtains today. The radical nature of this most recent crisis makes possible a recognition that the successes and failures of human knowledge now require the elaboration and exercise of a new kind of thought, one capable of expanding its theoretical and practical possibilities on a universal scale. This new species of thought is what Ortega designated "historical reason." In my opinion, Ortega's work—and especially the following pages—amounts to the postulation and in addition the living practice and demonstration of this richer kind of thought. No less, reader, is at issue here.

Paulino Garagorri

Historical Reason
(Buenos Aires, 1940)

1

My subject? The 1916 lecture course. "Ideas and Beliefs" and "Notes on Thought." Philosophy is a circular reality. Two human behaviors: having ideas, inhabiting beliefs. Unreality and reality of Theory. The golden mean: sports. Scientific thought starts from principles. Philosophical progress is not cumulative; it consists of a progressive backward movement to the roots of principles. Descartes's *Anábasis*.

I AM ESPECIALLY GRATEFUL for the introductory words of my friend of long standing, my colleague, my almost compeer, Professor Ravignani. I wish my thanks could be more profuse, but there is no time, no time at all. There is so much to say. So much I propose to say, and I have only four hourlong lectures at my disposal. This is the perfect opportunity to ignore the exordium. Let's leave it behind, presupposed and tacitly there. After all, my addressing this Faculty is not such an extraordinary event: This is my third visit; a few more—and it will be a daily occurrence.

What is my subject? My subject is—What else would it be? All that, everything that is the subject outside this hall, out there in the streets and squares, in the houses and casinos, in the clubs, bars, and taverns, in public meetings and secret government ones, in the worried man's solitude and in the fervor of crowds, on land, at sea, or in the air, in the stratosphere. That's the subject! But we will treat all that in a manner befitting this hall. In this place, from this Chair of Philosophy, we don't speak of *things*, but of what is *essential* about them. Although the air is scent-free, this is a Chair of Essences.

In contrast to the horror and suffering and passion that is the order of the day, here our subject will be, above and beneath the general distress, only what is essential to our day. According to mythological belief, as you know, it was the duty of fauns—those followers of terrible Pan—to howl prophecies and predictions from the fearsome depths of forests at those capable of disciphering their essential meanings.

When I published an article on the Roman Empire two months ago in *La Nación*—the first article, by the way, I had written in nine years—I had to apologize, when quoting Cicero, that I could only refer to a very meager text of one of his books, the only arsenal, the sole bibliographical weapon I had for entering the lists with the Roman Empire. Because for nearly a decade now I have had to wander the world without any books, which is rather like a turtle being forced to travel without his shell—.

Well, no sooner had the article appeared than a young Argentinian of exceptional promise, Máximo Etchecopar, lent me a fine edition of Cicero's complete works to consult during my stay.

Eager to reread the pages of Cicero in question, I was leafing along when I was struck by the following sentence, whose beauty certainly escaped Cicero when he wrote it. Cicero is gathering news of extraordinary things and events and, at one point, he says simply: "*Saepe etiam in proclis fauri auditis*" (Sometimes in battle, fauns' voices have been heard). Very well, in the thick of this infinite battle just joined, in the outdoors of space as well as in the indoors of the heart, we will bend our ear and attempt to make out the fauns' voices, roaring the impossible, the important, the decisive.

Our subject, then, is what is essential: the fact that man has once more lost his way in the world. But this is no chance happening; man has often lost his way before. What is more, what is more—as you will see—it is essential man lose his way, his way in the forest of existence. That is his tragic destiny and his distinguished privilege!

Several weeks ago Dr. Alberini astonished me—my old friend Alberini, "old" in friendship, not age. He astonished me by placing in my hands an exquisitely bound stenographic text of the lecture course I gave before this Faculty in 1916. I had no inkling of the existence of any record of those lectures; I had not kept a single page or note. But Dr. Alberini, who, along with other outstanding qualities, also has the alert eyes of a hawk, fit to decry the minutest event here below, recently learned of the existence of a stenographic copy of my first course. And since, in addition to farsightedness, the hawk has sure talons, Dr. Alberini soon laid his on that mass of paper and assured its preservation.

Now then, all I retained of those lectures was a memory—and what I recalled of the text was its having been completely forgotten. I confess I was considerably moved to find that there in the text—I gave the course nearly twenty-five years ago in this hall—in attempting to define man's peculiar condition I (rather, the "old" young man friends called by my name) said that man has the spiritual dynamics of a released arrow that has lost sight of its target.

I take pleasure and a certain pride, after nearly a quarter of a century, in being able to completely concur with that youthful turn of phrase. All the more so because the phrase, which back then must have seemed mere words or a curious image, has since been taken up quite literally by the most rigorous philosophers of the day.

Yes, man in truth, as my metaphor held, is formally pure movement, without figure or image, and movement drawn forward by a goal. And, for certain essential reasons, this entity *man*, whose sole reality consists in heading for a target, is all at once—in the end, perhaps always—bereft of a target, but nevertheless still propelled forward. Whither? Where does one go when one is directionless? What trail does one take when lost? What track when turned aside? For at least thirty years man has been aware of living under the shadow of a terrible lack of direction.

In truth, all the above are forms of not knowing what to do. Of course, these forms often wear strange disguises. For instance, throughout the world people are engaged in frenetic activity, drugging themselves with inauthentic hyperactivity in order to fill the vacuum of *not knowing what to do;* and at the other end of the scale are the complete do-nothings, with their attitude of quiet desperation, of self-abandonment to the rushing course of events.

That's just it. In politics no one knows what to do. Is that unusual? Is anyone surprised? The same is happening at the other extreme, at the opposite pole from politics: the physicist, faced with a similar situation in his discipline, doesn't know what to do in physics; nor the mathematician what to do in mathematics; and when the logician sees the foundations of his age-old principles tremble, what is he to do with his "so-called logic," as one of its most brilliant contemporary practitioners, the Dutch mathematician Brouwer, phrased it?

So as to round out the present course of lectures, and to sidestep certain topics difficult for a listening audience to grasp—there will be difficult material enough nonetheless—I have arranged to have published, simultaneously with these lectures, two of my works that you will do well to read if you want to be able to follow my thoughts exactly in these four lectures. One is the essay entitled "Ideas and Beliefs," shortly to appear in the Colección Austral; the other is "Notes on Thinking," to appear in the journal *Logos*, published by the Philosophy Faculty of this university. In the latter work

I deal with what has been called "the present crisis in the foundations of physics, mathematics, and logic." I shall refer frequently to both essays in the course of my lectures.

As regards each of the topics of this course, I should have liked to set forth the basic points of my philosophy, for our current problems are a vivid illustration of it. Since, however, in so short a time I could not have sufficiently developed any topic but would have had to proceed with weak assertions that were grossly abstract, overly hermetic, the result would have been much too abstruse.

Or again, conversely, I might have treated a solitary topic at length, but philosophy is so hard to section; it is rather like an elastic loop that will stretch and contract but cannot be cut. That solitary topic would have been left hanging in the air. Like those towered, unreal, and attractive cities the clouds contrive to design, it would have lacked all foundation and, above all, an obvious place in the system of my thought.

This leaves us the choice of an intermediary position: in a series of brief theses I shall draw the entire floor plan of my intellectual mansion, but I shall deal more slowly and in greater detail with only one portion of it.

The approach to our subject matter will therefore be gradual. How to begin? If you want to draw a circle, you have to begin—arbitrarily—somewhere. And I call the starting point "arbitrary" because there is nothing in the nature of a circle or the points that make up its circumference that dictates that we begin at a specific place. Only some motive external to the circle—ease of execution, material necessity—can oblige us to begin at a particular point.

This is true of any geometrical figure that closes back on itself. It cannot be said to begin or end anywhere; at most we can speak of closure. No point on such a figure is first or last.

So if we take any one as the starting point, we discover, in noting it, that the others existed already, were prior to it; that, in fact, all other points on the figure came first. But the reverse is also true: the point where our circle closes on itself reveals that the rest of the circle comes after.

Generalizing, we can call any reality where this happens "circular." Philosophy is such a circular reality. The countless ideas of which it consists are grouped according to certain hierarchies, even according to certain strict hierarchies. Some may rest on and be supported by others. They will possess an order of their own irrespective of our whims; but philosophy lacks an order for beginning and ending. None of its ideas is first, and none last. Philosophy never begins with a specific idea that is not preceded by countless others, like cinematic frames—nor does it ever finish, as parties always must. Philosophy is a never-ending tale.

Therefore this circularity is unavoidable and when we undertake to inform others of philosophy it forces us to face a peculiar difficulty, because to impart information we have to start somewhere. Imparting information is telling it, and telling is a performance that begins with something and ends with something. There is thus an essential incongruity between philosophy and its exposition. This incongruity exists because when we begin with idea A—that is, impart a first idea—it has one meaning in terms of what follows but has not been said, but quite a different meaning when, the circuit of our ideas complete, we return and view it—so to speak—from behind. Obviously it will look very different then. This, I repeat, is unavoidable; but the student new to philosophy will do well to keep it in mind. Philosophy, in addition to being a circular reality, is the practice of ideas, of theory. No more, no less. What is contained in the words "no more, no less" is extremely important. I deal with it in the essay "Ideas and Beliefs," but I will quote from it here to provide a precise summary of my thoughts on the matter:

"The point is to ease the contemporary mind toward a clear notion of what perhaps constitutes the ultimate source of all our present anxieties and misfortunes, to whit: that after several centuries of continuous and fruitful intellectual activity, on which the very highest hopes were placed, man has begun not to know what to do with ideas. He dare not dispense with them entirely, for basically he continues to believe that the working of the intellect is a marvelous thing. Yet at the same time he has the impression that the role and position in human life assigned to everything related to the intellect does not at all correspond to what was envisaged as appropriate for the last three hundred years. What then should the role and place of the intellect be? This is what no one knows." In order to settle this question, I was obliged to make a fundamental distinction that had not been made before, one that seemed to me obvious, between two modes of human behavior: *ideas*, a term that retains the meaning it has always had; and *beliefs*, in a very precise sense that, due to this very precision, makes it a completely new concept.

Beliefs are all those things that we absolutely take for granted even though we don't think about them. We are so certain that they exist and that they are just as we take them to be, that we never question them, but instead take them automatically into account in our behavior. When we go down the street we never try to walk through the walls of buildings; we automatically avoid bumping into them without ever having to think: 'walls are impenetrable.' At each moment, our life is supported by a vast repertoire of such beliefs. But there are also things and situations regarding which we find ourselves without a firm belief: we sometimes wonder whether certain things exist or not, whether they are one way or another. When this happens we have no alternative but to formulate an idea, an opinion regarding them. Ideas, then, are those "things" we consciously construct or elaborate, precisely because we *do not believe* in them. I think this is the best, the most precise, articulation of a possible answer to the momentous question of the peculiar and extremely subtle role ideas play in our lives. Notice that all ideas are thus described: commonplace ideas and scientific ones, religious ideas, as well as all other kinds. Because a reality is only complete and real to us when we believe in it. But ideas are born of doubt, that is to say, born in the empty space or hole vacated by a belief. This means that whatever evolves from an idea seems less than a complete and authentic reality to us. Then what are they? The orthopedic nature of ideas is easily perceived: they become useful when a belief has given way or weakened.

You will ask where these ideas and beliefs come from. Well, the origin of beliefs is obvious enough: beliefs are old ideas, often extremely old ones, sometimes as old as the human race. But that is just the point. They are ideas that have ceased to be mere ideas and have been compressed into beliefs. The vast majority of these beliefs operate within us without our realizing it. Even when we manage, in an exercise of our theoretical faculties, to turn them back into ideas, they continue functioning automatically as beliefs. Moreover, we can also go on believing in a belief that has been refuted in theory as an idea. An Idealist philosopher like Berkeley—whose theory asserts that matter is no more than insubstantial sense data—continues to act in the (nontheoretical) rest of his life as though matter were just matter, quite the opposite, in other words, of sense data.

The reverse also holds: ideas exist and function when we think them. At times they convince us, and we say they are "true." But "truth" is only a peculiar theoretical quality. It simply means that certain requirements specified by a theory have been met. Nothing more. "True" is all that an idea, a theory, can be. But this "all"—even if a lot—is much less than the automatically functioning *reality* of our beliefs.

I express this dual fact by saying that we have *ideas*, but we inhabit *beliefs*. Man always lives in the belief of *this* or *that*, and on the basis of these beliefs—which to him are reality itself—he exists, behaves, and thinks. Thus even the most skeptical of men is a believer, and profoundly credulous.

It surprises me that Christian theologians never thought of this notion of belief, which would have enabled them to arrive at a simpler, more solid concept of faith, and to have provided—for the first time, albeit in a onesided way—a concrete, controlable meaning for St. Paul's sublime phrase that "we move, live, and are" in Christ.

Similarly with our beliefs, whether they concern Christ sublime, or a lowly but impenetrable wall, or the solid ground under our feet, *in these* beliefs we move, live, and are.

If, in a short while, when you left this Faculty hall, you found no ground outside and instead nothing, your surprise would be great. Nevertheless, neither now nor at the moment of leaving the building would you have entertained the express idea that Viamonte Street was there with sufficient solidity for walking on; which would be proof you had taken the ground's presence for granted without having a discrete idea about it, without it occurring in the form of a thought or "idea."

To realize or be aware of something without counting on it is the most characteristic form of an idea; to count on something without realizing it, is the most characteristic form of a belief. Here, then, are two distinct modes of human comportment.

Let me repeat my formula in case you had difficulty grasping it the first time: to realize or become aware of something without counting on it—as happens with "centaurs"—is to have an idea; to count on something without thinking about it—as in my example of the ground beyond that door—is to inhabit a belief; and each is a discrete mode of behavior.

I am not in the least interested in any psychological explanation—obvious though they all are—that might be adduced to account for this difference. Such explanations only explain how it first appeared: that is, they reiterate the existence of these modes, which itself suffices as far as I am concerned.

Now, if beliefs are reality itself—since a belief in anything and that thing's being real for us are one and the same thing—it means that the stratum of our lives where beliefs hold sway is the most serious stratum of our lives; by comparison, all other strata are mere imaginary life and therefore totally lacking in seriousness, that is, in reality.

What I mean to suggest by this can be easily understood in the case of literature. While we are reading a novel we absent ourselves from our real lives but are present at—and all but participants in—the unreal life of the novel. While we read we did not live in all seriousness; on the contrary, we freed ourselves from the onerous and irrevocable seriousness of life and escaped into the realm of the imaginery that the novelist created for us. We should be thankful for novelists!

It is easy enough to see that in this sense literature is not a serious matter. Whenever we say this, however, writers tend to get cross; as we know, they are a *genus irritabile*.

But the same is true, to a lesser degree, of scientific truth and in general of all ideas. If, when compared with the truth of literature, scientific truth seems a serious thing, by comparison with lived belief, with credulous life, scientific truth itself is a less than serious matter.

In this way, I am able to push science and theory over in

the direction of literature. But there are additional reasons for this. And yet we avoid confusing science or literature with the unavoidable seriousness of life.

Literature and *science* belong to the unreal world of the imaginary. That's where they belong. That is their rightful place and their role. But the point of this is to highlight the following: it is imperative that we change our overly dramatic, unjustified attitude toward ideas, theory. A rectification is in order in this regard.

Besides other, graver forms of harm to which I alluded, this exaggerated respect for ideas puts significant obstacles in the way of learning science. This requirement of seriousness—that we believe in ideas—is a great trial to students. In the traditional way, which failed to distinguish between *ideas* and *beliefs*, it was and still is customary to expect students to believe in the existence of negative numbers. However, since it is impossible to believe in numbers, and since they are nothing but a combination of ideas, when the student tackles the problem this way, he cannot believe in them no matter how hard he tries, and so he is indirectly responsible for the obstacle to an understanding of what negative numbers mean in terms of mathematical theory. Finally, tired of the vain attempt to believe, one day the poor student gives up and lets the whole matter drop. Then, free of anxiety—and in a lighter frame of mind—he realizes that all he has to do with negative numbers is grasp what they amount to in the theory of mathematics, and nothing more.

"Well, what do you know?" he says to himself. "If I'd only known it was just talk. . . ."

That is understating things a bit; but if it isn't quite "just talk," it *is* just thought. What the student realizes is that negative numbers only exist within the conventions of mathematics, and that therefore they aren't to be taken seriously; there aren't, for instance, any negative apples. . . .

Then he feels liberated, feels he is master of an intellectual delight, a species of new and unexpected skill with which
to pursue the study of mathematics. Quite true; the spirit
in which we approach theory is not the one in which we
face the frightening reality that life ultimately and constitutionally is.

In the above I have taken pains not to use the word "game."
Perhaps it would have clarified the question. But I avoided
it because in this case it would have overshot the mark; it
would have been the wrong word.

No! Thoughts, ideas are not just a game. Thinking, theory, is not playing with ideas. Just remember, after all, that
the beliefs, which create the weighty and irrevocable reality
of the seriousness of our lives, first originated as thoughts.
Thinking is no game. Games are without responsibility; they
create nothing, but only serve to pass the time. Thought,
on the other hand, gives birth to world-views and life-visions
that, once they become beliefs, will be like vast continents
for man to inhabit, often for centuries.

Thinking makes human life possible because it allows man
to imagine the future and confront it. If suddenly all interpretations of the world were excised and we were left with
no knowledge of what might happen tomorrow—not even
the vaguest notion—the terror of it would overwhelm us.
Thus thought makes tomorrow possible, and tomorrow is
time itself. Far from being merely a way of passing time,
thought creates time.

When we theorize and deal in ideas, let us stick to a middle path between the overbearing seriousness of life, of living, and the irresponsible triviality of play. This middle path
is *sports*, which combines the strenuous effort of *living* with
the pleasurable attitude we adopt vis-à-vis *play*.

Plato tells us—and here Plato's unruly disciple Aristotle
agrees—that philosophy is, in his formal definition, the *science of free men*. Or to translate it so as not to lose the nuance

this word had in Athens, *the science of noble men*. Or to translate it even more exactly, because noblemen did not work, except perhaps in athletic competition, theory is *the science of sportsmen*.

Here is the spirit in which to confront ideas and theory. When we entertain them it must be with the ease, the joy, the skill, and the disinterestedness of the trained sportsman. To attempt to persuade or convince us of a theory, but without insisting that we believe it, is correct conduct for a thinker; it allows our minds the freedom of movement we need.

In our journey thus far we have advanced only two steps. With the first we announced that philosophy is a circular reality; in the second we said that it is theory, a working with ideas. I next pointed out the appropriate demeanor for handling ideas, for theory and philosophy. To this end I included a brief account of my distinction between *ideas* and *beliefs*. But now it is time to take a further step, a third one that will link up with the other two. If philosophy is *circular* and is *theory* then it is *circular theory*.

Now then, all other theories, all other sciences are more or less rectilinear and not circular. Therefore it turns out that as *theory* philosophy is an odd creature, quite unlike other sciences in intellectual design. And at once this brings to the fore a host of questions.

Is philosophy a *science* or not? If not, is it something more or less than science? And what is it? For the moment let us evade these question marks, which thrust their great, curved, seductive profiles in our direction like long swan's necks, dangerous as nooses, menacing as whips. . . .

Because our immediate task is to clarify the difference in the intellectual designs of philosophy and science. The sciences, as a group, the so-called "individual sciences," as Aristotle already referred to them, take their departure from commonsense notions that are found in the public mind and are held to be true. Usually these notions are contemporary beliefs, holding sway in the society and epoch in which a particular science arises. Our sole interest at this point is to observe that no science ever stops to question whether or not its principles are ultimately true; it never broaches the point. The truth of these principles is assumed in the way the truth of a soldier's service record is.

By bracing itself against these principles, scientific thought derives its *theorems and laws*. From these, in turn, it extracts further theorems and new laws, so that, starting out from its principles, scientific thought marches forward to conquer ever-new territories where problems exist. The sciences, in their forward march, add the truths of today to the conquests of yesterday without having to abandon the latter; that is, they accumulate truths. This is how they grow in our eyes, always occupying more space. To the untrained eye it seems that the sciences make progress. In a favorite old Spanish musical one of the stock characters, a Madrid low-lifer sings: "Today it's really striking, how science is getting ahead. . . ." And this popular perception of the progress of science shows that the actual march forward that constitutes scientific thought is highly visible.

But philosophy enjoys a different kind of locomotion; it never accepts an opinion as given and self-sufficient. Its inherent disposition is precisely to verify the solidity of its first principles. That is, it never trusts established or received opinion, whether it originates in science or the public mind. No! it demands much more. . . . In attendance at the birth and rebirth of philosophy there is always only one Good Fairy, and she is the ugliest of all: Doubt. Doubt is consubstantial with philosophy, but remember—Doubt addressing itself to concrete, forthright opinion. In a later lecture we will explain this qualification.

So that the first task of philosophy must be a critique of the principles of all opinion that passes as fundamental and definitive in science or the public mind. It needs, it assumes the responsibility of having man live according to principles that are ultimately solid and certain. To this end philosophy moves among principles, not to start out from them, but so as to dismember them, to examine their anatomy, and, if they survive this first operation, to test them and find them a more solid foundation; that is, to search beneath supposed principles for stronger ones.

In other words, philosophical thought, whose sole occupation is to assure the soundness of principles, must always be on the lookout for another, more fundamental principle behind the one at hand; or, to put it another way, philosophy is always marching to the rear, always in retreat. This is why, for all philosophy's labor in the course of time, it will never increase its mass; instead it works a constant and radical self-correction. This accounts for the impression of naïveté that surrounds the history of philosophy when viewed from the outside. It appears that instead of progress, philosophy is always making mistakes and always having to rectify its position. Philosophers, it is said, can never agree on essentials the way physicists and mathematicians can. In reality this is not what happens. On the contrary, if we return to the beginning of all the sciences in Greece, the subsequent history of philosophy is more coherent and continuous than that of any other science. Philosophy makes greater progress than any other science, although this progress is not exactly cumulative. Nor could it be; inasmuch as its subject is principle itself, there is no reason why today it should have a larger mass than it did a thousand years ago. Its ambition is to have a better principle today than yesterday. But a better principle is a different principle, and this is why philosophy always has to begin again. This is why it never bulks larger; it works hard enough but does not accumulate answers.

Philosophy, then, is never a question of progress by means

of continual additions. The progress of philosophy seems, for this reason, discontinuous: it doesn't describe the ever-wider circles that mark science's progress, but instead establishes a new center around which a new circle can be drawn. Each new principle, a minute yet elastic point, allows everything to appear in a new light. All at once the horizon of life is pushed back in all directions, creating a new horizon. Both progress and the history of philosophy proceed by means of a series of suddenly dazzling circles. This is the mode of existence, of doing and advancing, of human thought.

Here we have the origin of the philosopher's curious status. If his discipline consists in never accepting any opinion, whether derived from science or the public mind, it means that he must withdraw from public opinion, retire from the social world, which is first and foremost a web of public opinions. To the philosopher these opinions are all idols, *idolos forí*, "idols of the marketplace," as Bacon said.

The philosopher must not be bound by them. This is why philosophy is a retreat, an *anábasis*—to use a word that served as title for Xenophon's classic, *The Retreat of the Ten Thousand*. Of course these words are an incomplete translation of the Greek word *anábasis*. For *anábasis* is not just "retreat" but also "decline" and "descent." And, in fact, what General Xenophon recounts is how he was forced, along with an army of Greek mercenaries led by Cyrus the Younger, to fight Xerxes I, the Great Lord of Persia; how in defeat they retreated with enormous difficulty, making their way down among hostile tribes, from the high plateaus of Persia to the Mediterranean Sea. This is why the famous book ends with that classic scene—it has moved us ever since we were children—in which the surviving soldiers, in spite of exhaustion, finally manage to reach the peaks where they can see, far off, the sweetly fluttering flag of Greece, their homeland. And in the frenzy of their enthusiasm they cry out: *"Thalassa! Thalassa!"* (The sea! The sea!).

Well, in a similar sense philosophy is an outstanding *retreat* and famous *anábasis*. The philosopher, in retreat from the world, reminds us why the life of Descartes, who lived in retirement from everything and everyone, is and will always remain the paradigm of the philosophor's life: he retreated from his homeland and went to live in Holland. Why? He says that in Holland people disturbed him as little as trees in a forest. Descartes was in retreat from the culture of his day, that is, from the public opinion of his day and from the opinions held at the Sorbonne. *"J'ai quitté entièrement les lectures,"* he says; a peculiar confession for an intellectual! "I gave up reading completely." Exactly: Descartes read very little. But don't imitate Descartes only in that. He even withdrew from the rooms in which he lived, withdrawing into himself. This was so extreme that even his contemporaries started a joke about Mr. Descartes being "Mr. d'Ecart," Mr. Apart.

This retreat from public opinion places the philosopher in an essentially anachronistic light. For if his life is dedicated to retreat from public opinion, since public opinion is *social custom, intellectual custom* (public opinion is only what people think) and since custom is slow to establish itself (custom forms slowly), invariably, by the time a custom has finally become established as collectively dominant, the mental habits that went with it will have dried up and become outdated, and the philosopher will already be under the influence—whether he wants or not—of a new image of the world and of life.

Therefore, it is unfortunate but true: *public opinion* and *philosophy* are always out of step with each other. Public opinion is always behind the times, while philosophy is always premature.

This is what causes the philosopher's traditional and well-known *facies*, which is usually referred to as his being cold and bland. In fact it is impossible to excite him—remember, I do not say *interest* him—with problems that, willingly or not, he has left behind. But thanks to this, to his serenity amid the hurly-burly, in retreat he prepares for the future.

In an excellent treatise on ethnography, which your own Dr. Dujovne finished translating a few months ago, I learned that in the culture of the Zuni tribes—a charming, primitive people living in New Mexico who form part of the tribal federation ethnographers call Pueblo Indians, that is, they are the "people"—in Zuni culture, the orderliness of the universe depends on the priests' strict observance of their spiritual duties, and that the primary, the most important, of these duties is . . . never to get angry. If they did, the world would tilt on its axis. And a woman who has studied these peoples tells an anecdote that has affected me quite a bit: "One summer," she recalls,

> a Zuni family of my acquaintance lent me a house to live in, but because of rather complicated circumstances, another family claimed the right to use the house themselves. Once when the ill feelings had reached a high point, Quatsia, owner of the house, and her husband were in the main room with me when an unknown man began cutting down the flowering shrubs that remained in the corral. Now, it is the prerogative of the owner of a house to clear the corral of edible weeds, and so the unknown man was invoking his right to occupy the house by using the situation to make a public display of his claim. He never entered the house nor challenged Quatsia or Leo, who were inside; he simply went about slowly cutting down the shrubs. Inside Leo sat peacefully against a wall chewing on a leaf. Quatsia, on the other hand, got red in the face. "This is an insult," she told me. "That man out there knows that this year Leo is priest and isn't allowed

to get angry. So he is shaming us before the whole village by clearing out our corral." At last the intruder swept up the dried weeds, looked with pride around the corral, and then took himself home. Not a word was ever exchanged.

This not getting angry, this serenity without which, it is true, no one could invent the future, is why one of the most-often repeated words in the *Discourse on Method* is the word *repos* in a technical, not a grammatical, sense, especially if we include its synonyms such as *loisir*. Throughout his life Descartes made sacrifices so as to obtain *repos*.

Anyone who studies his Descartes, knows it really well, will know what this repose meant. Descartes knew full well how rare and difficult it was for a man to be able really to think, that is, think what he called "clear and distinct ideas." That is, *reason*—and it is still all too infrequent that one manages to do it. The rest of our being conspires to cloud the mental retina where the near-miraculous chemistry of thinking the evident takes place. . . . A passion for anything makes the mind murky, and so in order to make it clear Descartes wrote his *Treatise on the Passions*. Repose is a methodical freeing oneself of passion, and it constitutes, in a strictly formal sense—as I show in the aforementioned *Notes on Thinking*—the first and primary rule of his method, even though for various reasons it does not appear in the *Discourse* but in the famous letter to the Palatine princess. Parenthetically—and I say this as a wager and a challenge—the *Discourse on Method* has not yet been completely understood. It radiates Cartesian repose. It may seem like egoism—call it what you will—but the fact is that humanity has lived off that egoism for two and a half centuries, both morally and materially, because Descartes's thought, engendered in repose, gave birth to the modern technology in which "we move, live, and are."

I discover I have completely exhausted the agreed-to time

for this lecture (to have asked for more time would have been a serious trespass on your attention) just as we were about to round the first doctrinal corner of philosophy. For we were just going to examine the *reason* for this *retreat*, above and beyond the formal reason that consists in philosophical thought's peculiar advancing motion.

But let us stop now, so as to begin our second lecture at this point.

2

Summary. Metaphor. Philosophy as retreat toward fundamental reality. The substantialist thesis: things independent of me. Descartes's critique reduces it to a theoretical hypothesis. A critique of his critique for not being radical enough, in four parts. One: because he still retains the notion of being as what is independent of me. Two: because thought is not immediately available to itself. The fundamental "given": my coexistence with things. The independence of one from the other is mere theory, not fundamental principle. The fundamental "given" is human life.*

A MISTAKE as to the time it takes to get things said, one I almost never used to make but often make now, was responsible for my conveying to you in the previous lecture only about half of what I had intended to say. This left the first lecture with only one wing and the other cut off, which has disturbed the relation between each of the successive lectures and its corresponding topic. However, what really matters is that by the completion of all four we shall have managed to cover in more or less summary form all the announced topics.

*[Parts three and four were discussed in the third lecture. Ed.]

Taking a departure from the distinction between *ideas* and *beliefs*, the other day I suggested that in a sense theory is not serious, that it is never a matter of believing or not, but merely a question of whether "certain ideas" connect with "certain other ideas" and these with a "certain state of affairs." This is an enterprise in which only the portion of ourselves called "the intellect" is exercised.

To ask us to believe the Theory of Relativity has always seemed to me a distracting, an extraordinary, bit of nonsense. All the Theory of Relativity can do is persuade us, and that affects only our intellectual apparatus and nothing more. There is no reason why we should have to believe the Theory of Relativity. The fact that our intellect is central to the economy of our lives only means it is one more element of our being. The Theory of Relativity persuades us because it is true. And it is true because it meets certain criteria that the theory establishes in order to be correct on its own terms. No more and no less! This is what I said.

Beliefs—that is, all that we take for granted, willingly or not—form the awesome and irrevocable stratum of seriousness that human life ultimately and constitutionally is.

Scientific truth, by contrast, *theory*, like literature, belongs to the unreal realm of the imaginary. The serious part of theory is its application, its praxis. In principle, all theory is practicable; but theory by itself is unreality and imagination. This is why the appropriate mein to adopt for theorizing is not the overwhelming seriousness needed for living, but the halcyon joviality of sports. If there is any problem about understanding this point, it is due to our neglect of the fact that the most fervent of contemporary man's beliefs is his belief in reason, his faith in the intellect, in science.

People often say nowadays, frivolously and without sufficient knowledge, that faith in reason is on the wane. In my *Notes on Thinking*, soon to appear in the journal of this Faculty, I attempted a complete diagnosis, the most complete one now possible, of the present status of Western man's belief in reason.

There is no doubt in my mind that such a belief persists. But it is one thing to believe in reason and quite another to think we should believe the ideas reason engenders. It is one thing to have faith in science, and quite another to insist we believe the particular theories that science generates.

Notice there would be a flagrant contradiction in our believing, at one and the same time, in reason and its ideas and in science and its theories. One cannot be reconciled with the other.

If one believes in science, one believes—takes for granted—that man is always capable of creating theories; that, given the known facts at a particular moment of history, those theories will be as true as possible; and that, therefore, we will have ever more precise, more comprehensive, more certain theories.

Now, if someone put his or her faith in Newton's theory, then when it was undercut by the relativity theory of Einstein—and this is the least prejudicial example since in this case the theory was not *disproved*—that person would have lost faith in Newton's theory and in reason as well.

A belief in science does not require us to believe in its changing theories, but only be persuaded by them. This led us to a comparison of the intellectual progress of philosophy with that of the sciences.

The *sciences* depart from principles supposed to be true and move forward, accumulating truth upon truth. *Philosophy*, on the other hand, the aim of which is to gain solid ground—the "certainty of the principle," to use a Platonic expression—moves ever backward, inasmuch as its task is to search out beneath yesterday's supposed principle today's more certain one, a more principal principle. What counts is to attain and verify the *more* certain principle beneath today's supposedly certain one. For this reason, because it "advances" to the rear, philosophy is not accumulation but adjudication. It is not a circle that becomes larger in the manner of scientific progress, but rather the new center for another circle in which we suddenly begin to see things in a new light. Philosophy, therefore, proceeds in method and direction by a series of sudden illuminations. Philosophy, the center of thought and, therefore, the human center of human life, continually changes its venue and does so in a backwards direction. Philosophy—let us say it in French— *marche à recoulons* and consists in making us realize that in science, as in life, when you leave you always unwittingly leave behind what is most important.

With each new stage in philosophy, the human intellect takes another step to the rear; instead of stretching out, it draws in. This is the same crouching movement the tiger makes when preparing his predatory leap. It is like the hand drawing the bow. Thanks to it, the arrow acquires its thrust and will rush to pierce a distant mark.

Man, including the man in the street, even including Mass-Man, whose disdain for the philosopher is so great—the Mass-Man and the philosopher share an innate mutual dislike— man, whomever he may be, is oblivious to the fact that he is impelled, enchanted, supported in his living by a philosophy that stands quietly behind him. Just as when an arrow is released the hand pauses by the ear. But the arrow, which loses sight of its target, also forgets the releasing hand. The arrow is flying ingratitude.

All this is only metaphor. But today the only philosophers who shy at metaphor are the provincial ones. The most recent, most rigorous studies of logic have discovered, both with surprise and cause, that language never meshes perfectly with ideas; that, therefore, every expression is metaphor, that the *lógos* itself is a phrase. For if what we say does not coincide with what we think, then it only suggests it. And a *saying* by *suggestion* is one way to define metaphor.

Brouwer, the brilliant mathematician who gave logic its last great push forward, said recently that mathematics is entirely independent of mathematical language. Notice we speak here not of natural language but of the symbolic languages of algebra and logic, with their pretention to absolute exactness.

After all, this was exactly what Pierre Boutroux—not the philosopher but his son, the excellent mathematician—maintained in 1920 in *The Scientific Ideal of Mathematics* when he wrote: "The mathematical fact is independent of the logical, algebraic clothing with which we try to represent it."

Indeed, the idea we have of a mathematical fact is far richer and more pregnant than all the definitions of it we can give, or than all the forms or combinations of signs or propositions with which we can express those definitions.

Similarly, what Newton's rival, Huyghens, termed a *light wave* is a metaphor in comparison with the *liquid wave* of water. But Louis de Broglie's wave, the *quantum wave*—basis of today's physics—is even more metaphorical because it is not a wave of water, nor of ether like the light wave, but a *probability wave*. Now then, a *probability wave* is decidedly metaphorical.

"The wave," de Broglie wrote in 1929 in his "Determinism and Causality in Contemporary Physics," published in *Revue de Métaphysique* when his marvelous discovery was still quite new,—"the wave is not a physical reality but only the symbolic representation of the positions and the stages of movement of a molecule."

Now then, this is metaphor: a symbolic representation. Why, as long ago as 1886 the great Bergson put it elegantly when he said: "Thought is incommensurate with language."

It is rather embarrassing to have to repeat what is old hat nowadays, but it is imperative that we overthrow the intellectual "provincialism" that hobbles the spirit in not a few countries.

Ladies and gentlemen, one of the things dying in the world today is provincialism. All varieties, even the most illustrious—because there have been and still are illustrious kinds of provincialism. But we will take up this line another time. (A very slight hint of my intent here can be found in that old book of mine, *The Revolt of the Masses*.)

But our present concern is to give the precise reason why philosophy always moves backward, why its progress is a perpetual retreat. The reason is this: we live according to certain ideas—which are more or less beliefs—about what reality ultimately is. Why so? Because life is immersion in the hurly-burly of things. Now, not only are these legion, we are not only surrounded by innumerable things, but in addition they are grouped differently according to their degree of reality.

That is, a stone is different from a number because it is a stone and the number a number, but also because the *stone*'s way of being real is different from the *number*'s way. This is so to such an extent that even while we realize that the number is *something*, we doubt if, in comparison with a stone, it makes any sense to say the number *is real*; in any case, we say its reality is different but still somehow real. And so with everything else.

There are ghosts and solid bodies; there are mirages and there is real water; there is the body and its shadow. So that we are obliged not only to study things, as does science, but also to know something about their reality or unreality and, within the compass of the real, how to rank them according to their reality.

For ghosts do not entirely lack reality, although they seem less real than our bodies. Even the centaur and the chimera, fantastic creatures indeed, must have a degree of reality since we are not completely at liberty to imagine them. A centaur without a man's torso is as impossible as a round square or a man with no torso—which means that this multitude, of both things and their way of being real, forces us to seek a larger reality that will serve as a benchmark for measuring all other realities, so we can award them their place and degree of reality, locate them in an ontological hierarchy, fit them into being.

Our lives rest on this larger—or, as I prefer to call it, *radical*—reality. Our lives differ according to our belief as to what constitutes this radical reality. Our life will be different according to whether we think with rigor, or believe with devotion, that the greatest, most fundamental reality to which all others can be reduced is matter, or instead that the basic reality, the *ens realissimum*, is God.

Now, we usually speak of *philosophy* as the theory charged with explaining the nature of this radical reality and with defining other realities in terms of it. In the seventh book of *The Republic*—precisely where Plato gives his eloquence free rein in order to tell us his classic myth of the *cave*—he says: "Man must go in search of a stronger being, a being that is more being," and he adds that this search is *philosophy*. Similarly, Aristotle has philosophy proper consist in the science of being qua being, of the real as such.

In the preface of a recent edition of *Encyclopedic Dictionary* I draw attention to Western man's particular clumsiness in naming his sciences. Almost all their names are grotesque and absurd and rarely tell us what the science is about. Yet no discipline has suffered more than our own from the ridiculousness of its name. Just imagine: *philosophy* equals *lover of Sophia*. Can you imagine anything more vulgar? Imagine this: *philosophy* equals *lover of wisdom*. Can you imagine anything more imprecise?

Nevertheless, this human occupation, with its unfortunate name, is charged with deciding what *radical reality* is. This decision is a thought that proposes *some-thing* as radical reality; therefore, it makes a radical proposal or thesis. And the history of philosophy is divided into two vast epochs, each governed by its own thesis.

The first radical thesis, involving ancient Greece and its Medieval descendants—excepting the theological idea of God—proclaimed the *world* or *nature* as the radical reality. Or, to put it otherwise, according to this thesis the *world* is what really is. The *world*, nature, is a great big thing made up of many small things. But, great or small, the "thing," the "*res*," and, ultimately, the "physical thing," is the *prototype* of being according to this way of thinking.

And since the vocabulary of philosophy was invented at that time, the mode of being exemplified by "things," by the "*res*," was named *reality*.

However, there are not only "things." There is also change, of which movement is the most obvious example. But visible movement was always presented as the movement of some "thing." In movement the "thing" changes place but never seems altered; when the movement stops, the "thing" is just as it was before, identical. For this reason, the *res* seemed a necessary presupposition and a condition for movement, because you never have the latter without the former and, so it seemed to the Ancients—using observation—things could remain still, unmoving. Moreover, movement is easy to see but difficult to conceptualize. Thinking about movement gave the Greeks vertigo, and it has this effect on us too. The truth is that once Greek thought became entangled in Zeno's arguments against the reality of movement, it could never free itself. For these two reasons—and for many others—"things," and especially motionless "things," remained the prototype of being. But notice that this "thing" or exemplary reality is an entity. Greek ontology consists in the analysis of the way entities are, the way they appear to us. This analysis resulted in the categories, not, that is, the classification of what beings there are, not of things, but of the mode of being of those things.

For example: a color cannot exist without an entity to make possible its extension. By itself, in isolation, the color could not exist. There must be an entity to support its existence. Therefore the being of the entity is a greater and prior reality than the being of color. Color is not, then, *sensu stricto*, a "thing" but merely the quality of a thing. Its mode of being, which depends on a real thing existing in its own right, is termed *substance*, and so forth and so on. It would not be germane to pursue this point today; in the next lecture we will return to it in more detail. Suffice it to say now that, because a visible entity was the model for deciding the cardinal attributes of reality—a visible entity, the "thing," the *res* par excellence for the Greeks—all other entities, even if judged less than "things," were still understood to possess some fraction of those attributes; thus the sublime and ultramundane Platonic "Ideas" were thought to retain much of the character of things, as Aristotle's forms and even souls—the most subtle of all forms—were considered quasi-things. Presently you will see why, in my view, the quasi-thing, soul, which is supposed to be a product of spiritualism, is really a remnant, vague yet nevertheless a remnant, of materialism, of corporealism.

For the ancient Greeks, then, the primordial characteristic of real and absolute being is *what is there*, independent of ourselves. And, more generally, each thing—that really is a *thing*—is independent of every other thing. While they may mutually influence each other, their being, their reality, does not depend on this influence. For the Greeks, therefore, *reality* is, in the fullest sense, what *is for itself*. This is why the idea of a *created being* or a *creating being* would never have occurred to a proper Greek. This is why it could never have occurred to a proper Greek that there could be any being—any creature—whose being had its origin in another being, or a being—God—who like a magician brings forth from himself creatures different from himself. (Notice that in what I

have said there is nothing that formally contradicts the idea
of creation. I merely offer a graphic illustration of a proper
Greek's inability to understand a *created being* and a *creating
being*.)

If we had time, we could examine just how far in this
direction a decidedly sublime Greek intellect was able to
go—a privileged Hellenic mind, although living among Jews.
(To an extent this mind was the disciple of a brilliant Hebrew
philosopher: Philo of Alexandria, a man whose influence on
the history of thought has far outstripped the popularity of
his name.) This latter-day Greek—an authentic one, nevertheless—was Plotinus.

One gathers that Plotinus wanted to conceive of something like God's creation of worlds and things, but . . . he
simply could not! He was not able to! And so instead he
decided that things, the world, were not God's creations
but His emanations.

The difference between the two concepts is clear. They
are quite different. (Here we must excuse Saint Thomas of
Aquinas, who defines creation—it must have been a lapse—
with the word "emanation.") In creation, the *created being*
has a being entirely distinct from the *creating being*, since to
say man is made "in the image and likeness of God" is simply a gentle way of telling us that we are "infinitely different
from Him"; on the other hand, the *emanated* being has the
same being as the *emanating* one; it is his radiation and nothing more.

Plotinus' God is the *ens exuberantissimum*, the *exuberant* one,
the *superabundant* reality, the being with too much being;
and for this reason he overflows—as Plotinus says—he
exceeds himself, flows, emanates. This left-over part of the
divine being, this superfluous reality, is the world, and ourselves, mankind.

How could a proper Greek, a true Greek, conceive of the
idea of creation if what he already thinks is being, at its

most authentic, possesses as a basic attribute the most fundamental attribute of God and the one most antithetical to creation?

Indeed, for Aristotle the world is made of matter and forms *sensu stricto*, which are eternal. In a universe of eternal things, a creative God would be out of work. And one has to admit that, in truth, Aristotle's God is very nearly a do-nothing.

Let me say parenthetically that although it seems strange, philosophy—except for a brief instant with Schelling—has never made a serious attempt to think through, and on its own terms, the idea of creation.

But it would be a mistake, it would be wrong to think that philosophy will never choose as its peculiar task the analysis of the idea of creation; for even when considered solely from a philosophical point of view, it is a splendid idea. But all this is leading us astray.

What I wanted to establish at this point was simply that for Greek and for Medieval philosophy, *being*, in the strictest sense, is *independent* being, on its own and for itself.

Other aspects of the thesis that the world is the fundamental reality may occupy us tangentially in later lectures. But now we must observe, in haste, the birth of the other great thesis, inaugurated by Descartes, in which we have been educated: the thesis that holds that the fundamental reality is *thought*, the *idea*, *idealism*. Equally, this will be an excellent example of the essentially—essentially—retrograde movement of philosophical thinking.

According to Aristotle the being of *color* could never have the value of a *primordial being*, since color needs some object on which to extend itself; therefore, it needs the support of something else. The reality of color is not independent; it depends on *things*. A *thing* antedates its *color*; it is behind or beneath its color, as its sub-stance; in other words, it is its *principle*.

We all remember how Aristotle never tires of reiterating

the primordiality of substantial being, of substance: "Substance comes first of all, in order of concept, knowledge, and time."

Very well! But what happens is this: these things that are substances—this horse, this man, in Aristotle's examples—may well be more real than their qualities, than their capacity, than their relationships, and may be, in comparison with other categories of reality, the strongest being, the *most masterly* reality *(kyriótata)*, as Aristotle says. But all I have to do is close my eyes, and this horse, this selfsame horse, or this selfsame man disappears without a trace. . . . It hasn't taken any time at all: or rather, only "the blinking of an eye—And yet it was time enough for these masterly realities to evaporate; or more; to be annihilated.

Of course, you will say when the "eye blinked," *they* were not annihilated, but continued to be real. Yet who says this? Who can assure me that the horse and the man I saw still exist, remain in existence, have substance when I don't see them?

Their subsistence above and beyond what I see is at least problematic. Add to this that sometimes I dream of horses, have horses that appear in my dreams—What about these horses? Are they real? Are they unreal? They are imaginary horses, dream horses: how could they be real!

Moreover, there are states of hallucination. So that my seeing something is no guarantee that it exists over and beyond my seeing it, nor is it any guarantee—it could be a hallucination—that what I see is really there before me. The horses in a hallucination, or the dream horse, seem to be there but are not. And since everything in the world reaches me through sensory perception, the reality of this world is, at the very least, a suspect reality, a doubtful reality. . . .

In a naïve text on Roman Law that was used forty years ago in an ancient, provincial Spanish university, the author begins the subject of Roman taxes by saying that "in Rome, taxes began by not existing." Very well; the reality—of which we were so certain—of horse and man, of things and their aggregate or world, turns out to be suspect, doubtful. For this reason it cannot aspire to the status of primordial reality. On the other hand, there is no question but that I *see* the horse, *see* the man. What is in question is not *my seeing* them, but they themselves. That is, the reality of the horse—at least the certainty of it—depends on my seeing it, but my seeing is independent of whether or not they exist. Therefore, the world is doubtful, but my own doubting (its reality) is not.

This is the well-known argument—perhaps, as we shall see, not well known enough—that Descartes conceived in his stove chamber: the argument that originates the second great thesis in the history of philosophy. (This thesis affirms the reality of thought, of the *cogitatio* or consciousness as the fundamental reality.) Because *seeing, hearing, dreaming, reasoning* are nothing but forms my thinking takes, what there really and absolutely is, according to Descartes, is *me* and *my doubt, me* and *my ideas, me* and *my thoughts*, which are all *modes* that *I am*. Thus, *I* am the only thing that really and primarily exists in the universe; *I* am the *universe.*

Now tell me if you think it makes any sense for us to believe such a paradox! Yet this paradox has been one of the great and subtle theories, one of the greatest and most subtle theories ever conceived by man.

Certainly not! A theory is not something we believe or do not believe. It is instead a question of whether or not certain ideas fit together, and whether they match the facts. Therefore, for Descartes, the world lacks reality, and the leading, the primary reality becomes the *I*.

The Cartesian critique of philosophical realism makes clear the fact that when one proclaims the *world* to be the fundamental reality, as in the first thesis, one forgets, leaves out, never takes into account, the very thought responsible for this claim—the one that presupposed the world as *independent being*.

When, with Descartes, we realize this, the world is reduced to a secondary reality, and *thought*—the *cogitatio*—acquires the status of the strongest, the most real being.

For antiquity, the extramental existence of the world was beyond question; it was reality itself. This is why the Ancients made it the first principle. But Descartes, with his line of reasoning, exposed the error of this supposed reality and its unquestionable status: the reality of a being independent of me is only hypothetical, a theory, our own construct. However obvious, however natural and plausible, it is still no more than a hypothesis.

This is the elegant, the magnificent intellectual feat credited to René Descartes. I can find no words to express my admiration for this gentleman who "dressed in black from head to foot" in the Spanish style. He was the clearest, the most penetrating, the keenest mind we have had in the Western world. But I must stick to my own message. And for now my message goes counter to his; even though mine ultimately amounts to praise of him.

Now the weighty part begins. I warn you that from here to the end of our lecture, the subject matter is difficult, and difficult to follow. I only hope this is the only lecture in the cycle that will be thorny, abstract in the extreme, difficult, unbearable. But there is no alternative and I can only beg to be forgiven for it.

In any case, comprehension will be enhanced if what I said in the previous lecture about theory is born in mind; in other words, that it is not "serious," not a question of believing it or not but of seeing whether the ideas fit together and match the facts to which they refer. In which case—mark this well—it is Descartes, and not I, who must look for a first truth about what is real, who is obliged to find something the reality of which is true without this truth being due to other supposed truths, any at all. To this end, he employs as his method a radical doubt, the suspension of our customary beliefs and truths. Now then, all Descartes's other ideas, and all our own ideas in criticizing him—since we agree to combat him on his own ground and with his own weapons—must follow the rule that in this first step we not use any previous truth for support. So be it.

Here, then, are four points into which for the nonce— one could add many more— I condense my critique of Descartes and, generally, of modern philosophy, which never left the magic circle drawn by his clear mind.

First point. From the fact that when I close my eyes the horse before me disappears, and that, inversely, when I dream I see nonexistent horses, Descartes infers that the reality of the horses is *problematic,* and not *fundamental* and *unquestionable.*

But here he has clearly been a little too hasty. From the fact that the horse disappears when I close my eyes one can only infer that when I don't see it, it may not exist, but certainly not that it doesn't exist when I do see it.

In such exasperatingly radical considerations as these— since we are seeking a first principle—we must take things as they present themselves and not deform them by the application of secondary theories. These can be as plausible and right-seeming as you please, but they are still only *theories;* whereas we seek a basis for all theory. For this reason, inversely, when I see *horses* in my dreams, it doesn't mean they don't exist, because dreaming is only a hypothesis we have created to make sense of this twin reality: what we see when asleep and what we observe when awake. The intellectual elegance, rigor, and panache of accepting only what is evident obliges us to invalidate, at least provisionally, our received theories. And, for this reason, it is surprising that Descartes did not do so.

Why shouldn't the world consist of things that exist while

I see them and cease to exist when I don't, but nevertheless *are* by themselves? I don't mean this is so, or that anyone should believe this. All I hold is that in this first step Descartes has no right to eliminate this possibility. Especially Descartes, who has just invited us to use his method of *radical* doubt and to suspend all received opinions. Could it be that Descartes was not as free as he supposed from the Classical-Scholastic ontology he tried to overthrow?

The chapter of *Méditations sur la philosophie première* in which Descartes carries out this analysis has the title, "Des choses que l'on peut révoquer en doute." Very well; it is not clear that one can "revoke in doubt" the reality of the horse that I see while I see it, unless, of course, by *reality* one understands precisely all being that is absolutely independent of oneself, as did the Ancients. *Seeing* the horse and its *being before me* or *there being a horse* are one and the same thing. What is more, it is already an incorrect and risky assertion to call "seeing" that which happens when I have a horse before me, because "seeing" is no more than a psychological hypothesis in rather dubious combination with a physiological hypothesis, which in its turn is combined with several hypotheses having to do with physics, and so forth.

But Descartes clings to a notion of *being*, of reality that he took over from Aristotelian Scholasticism. This is the notion that consists, as we saw, in only considering real what is absolutely independent of me. And naturally one may have doubts about that. . . .

Then, Descartes continues, although I can doubt the horse I see, and the world I see, I cannot doubt my own seeing, nor can I doubt the fact of my doubting, or, in general, my *cogitatio*, or thought. So that all there is finally and really is *myself and my doubt:* the world is abolished and man alone is left with his thoughts.

And so for the next three centuries *being, existence, reality*, in the widest sense, will mean that there is only *myself*. Thus we can, for the present, call idealism solipsism.

Second point. The reason Descartes doubts the reality of the horse he sees but not the reality of his seeing, the reason he doubts the reality of the world but not the reality of his doubt, is this: as we just saw, Descartes holds the belief, he continues in the belief, that reality must, willy-nilly, consist in what is absolutely independent of us. He accepts this as true. He never doubts it.

By the same token we have here a typical case of what I call *beliefs (creencias)*, and you will do well to keep this in mind for our next lesson. Remember that we caught Descartes out in a belief, in spite of the fact that he never owned up to it. This shows that we can detect the beliefs of our fellow men, whether or not we are their contemporaries; Descartes, moreover, does not make his belief here explicit. And this implies something even more basic: we can discover another man's beliefs even though he is unaware of the hold they have on him. This principle—which I hope to develop in the next lesson—is what permitted me to put the methodology of history on a new footing, in the hope that this admirable vocation called "history" can now stop being mere story-telling or, at best, excellent technique—admirable, necessary, highly respected but mere technique—and become true science.

But I was saying that Descartes believed that the real, the only real being, was what was absolutely independent of me. Now anything independent of me can only enjoy an accidental relationship with me. And for this relationship to exist there must be some intermediary between us. Now, the reality *world* is not immediate, but itself requires such an intermediary. An act of thinking, of "realizing," is necessary to mediate between reality and myself, to put us in relation to one another. Thought, on the other hand, is an immediate reality. For this reason I can doubt the world, because it is distant and not immediate; but it is senseless to doubt thought, which is as immediate as I am myself. Although he uses a different—not a more rigorous—terminology, this is the quintessential form that Husserl gives to Cartesian thought, purifying it with a phenomenology that loops-the-loop of idealism.

But the assertion that my thought is immediate is a complete error. This must be said, and I hope Descartes and Husserl, my teacher, will forgive me. When I see a horse, all there is is *horse*. The horse is in my presence, and that is that. My *seeing* is not an additional presence, also there (for me). I am not aware, or I am not conscious, of seeing, but only of the horse. To become conscious of my sight, a further act of awareness is required, by means of which I become aware that a moment before, I saw the horse. This new thought or act of awareness in which I realize I formerly saw a horse is a retrospective act. It is customarily called "remembering," with all the attendant and notorious chances for error that go with memory, which rival those of seeing. Husserl, employing a euphemism, calls this memory, this secondary act that immediately follows the primary act of my seeing, "retention." But beneath this euphemism there is only memory. From which it follows that my seeing is not aware of itself, that it is by no means certain that thought thinks itself, or is immediate to itself, but that, at most, one thought can think another thought, exactly the way it does a horse, or a triangle, or a centaur, or the world.

For idealism and, in general, for the whole modern era, the primary, fundamental, prototypical reality—what is really and absolutely—is an *I* thinking things. The latter, according to idealism, have no reality of their own, but only the reality of being thought; so that consciousness, the *cogitatio*, or thought, is simply my being aware of what I see, in other words, what ever since Kant has been called "content of consciousness," or, an awareness of my "content," of my own thoughts: in short, of myself.

But we have just seen that this will not wash; *sight* is not aware of its seeing; a *thought* does not *think itself*, cannot *think itself*. This means, clearly and simply, that this reality—consciousness, *cogitatio*, or thought—far from being reality, is only an invention, a hypothesis, a theory, and nothing more. Therefore, it cannot serve as primordial reality, the most real reality, inasmuch as it is only a pseudo-principle.

I maintain, then, that it is a falsification to describe the basic state of affairs of our relationship with things as consciousness or thought—that is, to believe that our primary relation with things is thinking them. What we call *seeing* is, pure and simple, having something present, there before us, having something in our presence. This is the plain state of affairs. *Seeing* is not part of this pure state. As we said earlier, *seeing* is simply an explanation that was dug up to explain the fundamental fact of having a horse before me. But that fundamental, "radical," state of affairs of my relationship with things is correctly described not as a thinking awareness (which ultimately would be the double awareness of myself and what I see), but as my unmediated encounter with things qua things; and not things *as thought*, not with thought of things; that is, the horse is a *horse* to me, and the flower a *flower*, and you are (for me) a patient audience, and (to you) I am what I really am to each one of you.

Indeed, it would be amusing to describe exactly what I know I am being to you, not each of you, since I don't know you individually, but rather what I know I am to each one of the different types of people I know you to be. Wouldn't it be worthwhile to dedicate a lecture to this topic one day? There is no question of its suggestiveness since I have only to mention it casually and in passing, for the first stirrings of a strange phenomenon—the first signs of uneasiness—to show in at least some faces. Why did certain of you begin to feel uneasy at the merest hint that I might say here and now what I am for the type of person you are? What is uneasiness? Here is another topic that could be the subject of a lecture.

However, the decisive point is that the fundamental event

of our relation with things can only be correctly described as the bare coexistence of *myself* with *things*. The *one* is just as real as the *other*, *myself* as much as *things*, except that *to be real* changes its meaning; and instead of meaning *independent* as before, it now means that each *depends* on the other: they are inseparable, each is for the other. Things are *to me* and I am *theirs*. I am given over to them: they surround me, sustain me, wound me, caress me. Between them and me there is, therefore, none of what is called consciousness, *cogitatio*, or thought. The primary relation that pertains between man and things is not intellectual, not a matter of *realizing* they are there, thinking them or contemplating them. If only it were! Instead it is being among them and with them; and, on their part, to be actually affecting me.

The realism of antiquity held that the reality of the world was independent of human thought. Modern idealism holds that thought is independent of the world. I say: an *independent world* or *independent thought* do not exist. They are merely two hypotheses, two theoretical constructions, and not reality. What is, primarily and in purest form, is the coexistence of man and world; this is what there is: the mutual existence of man and world, the world and man, man and the world, and so forth, without end . . . Like those pairs of divine beings that, according to the religion of ancient Greece and Rome, were destined to be born and to die together—the Dioscuri or Gemini—who were also called, for this reason, *Diconsentes*, the unanimous gods.

I proposed this metaphor and propounded this thesis back in 1916, and I have found it again in the typescript given me by Dr. Alberini. This thesis destroys the idealist position in general by attacking it on the very point with which Descartes brought it into existence and on what is today its most rigorous and pristine base, that is, by showing that Husserl's famous "phenomenological reduction" is clearly and simply impossible.

Well, the years have passed and I have developed this thesis a great deal more. When I have set forth the third or the fourth point of my critique of Descartes its vast prospects will appear. For it amounts to no less than a third fundamental thesis. Just as Descartes shows that the realism of antiquity—when it proclaimed the world, nature, as the fundamental reality—left out of account the thought of the man who presupposed them as independent being, so too did Descartes, when he proclaimed thought the fundamental reality, leave out of account man in his primary, unadorned coexistence with things, in his pre-intellectual relation with them, which is nevertheless a "having-to-do" with them. Now then, this being obliged to traffic with things from minute to minute instead of thinking about them is what we call living, human life. Behind nature lies thought, theory—but behind thought lies our simple, concrete, and dramatic life, the life of each one of us, forcing us to think and theorize: the absolute fact of mankind as the life of each person, as *my life*.

Thus, with this second point, and without it seeming especially important, we have gone beyond all idealism and set foot firmly outside that circle of ideas called "the modern era."

Here you have the result of our latest step backward, our most recent retreat. We can now make out, albeit faintly and at a distance, a brand new principle, the principle of the future: our ordinary, everyday life, the life of each one of us as the fundamental reality and principle of reason, as vital reason. *Thalassa! Thalassa!*

3

Summary and additions. "Being aware of something" and "consciousness." A reform of fundamental concepts. Three: Because doubt does not abolish reality; reality continues to oppress me with its doubtfulness. Four: Because doubt and theory are not without entailments; both contain their antecedents—the cause of the doubt, the decision to theorize. Methodological doubt is secondary compared with real doubt, and the "afterwards" is a "why." One philosophizes because one lives. The six prior theses that Descartes left out. What is life as fundamental reality? Purely and exclusively "event."

ONE OF THE FEW philosphical works of the Spanish sixteenth century to be written in the vernacular was published in 1517; its author was a certain Fernando Alonso de Herrera, who, in spite of a name as warlike and illustrious as that of any conquistador, was a modest professor at Alcalá University. What I enjoy about his book is its amusing title, written in an old Spanish not yet quite certain of itself. The title goes like this: *Short Argument in Eight Sorties Against Aristotle and His Followers.*

By "sorties" he meant attacks, charges. It was a military term. Well, the other day I was engaged in a similar undertaking; except that, instead of warring against Aristotle I struggled with Descartes. And, instead of eight sorties, my attacks or charges number four only.

In the last lecture, I gave two of the four points in which I sum up my critique of Cartesian thought—and, in general, of modern philosophy. In the first I showed that Descartes was right with respect to the fundamental thesis of Greece and the Middle Ages, which held that the "world of things" was primordial reality; that *being* or *reality* were what was absolutely independent and, therefore, quite independent of our minds. But we saw that this *reality* was neither self-evident nor beyond question: it was merely something that reason had supposed and not reality itself. On the other hand, Descartes was wrong to believe we can doubt things that are there before us.

As the second point, I set forth the thesis that Descartes substituted for the thesis of antiquity—and with which he set the limits for the entire modern era. Descartes's new thesis was that the unimpeachable and primordial reality is the *cogitatio*, or thought; and we saw how this, too, was an error.

Allow me to insist one last time on the second point because it is the exceptional and decisive one. (Besides, I want those especially interested in philosophy to pay particular attention.)

The bone of contention is the following: which is the most adequate term or designation for the primary relationship of man to things? Take, for example, the relationship of all of us to this room.

According to modern tradition, that relationship consists in our being aware of it. Let us provisionally accept this way of putting it, but request one clarification. For *to be aware of* or to realize can mean two quite different things: it can mean that this room is not only there, by itself, but that it is there for us, present to each of us, that this room is the precise room it is, as in the examples of the horse that was a *horse* to me and the flower that was a *flower* to me. In this sense, *to be aware of* means that what I declare "real" invades me, appears to me in its being. Or, to put it another way—which is the same but in reverse—that I really am in this room, that my *being aware of something real* is for me to be *in it*.

But according to another sense—the one it has in modern philosophy—my *being aware of* something has a quite different meaning. My *being aware of* this room, according to the modern idealism of Descartes, means that its image but not the room itself is present to me. What I am aware of, in other words, is my own mental state. Here *being aware of* something is being aware of something *mine, of myself*. Therefore, it is the opposite of my going out toward being, of it appearing to me; instead, it means confinement within my own mind; or as a latter-day Greek, who foresaw idealism, said: "Man lives in his thought as in a besieged city, from which he cannot escape."

This is the meaning of the term consciousness. *Consciousness* is, or is supposed to be, a reality that is aware of itself, something immediate to itself, pure reflexiveness.

In the ninth paragraph of his *Principles of Philosophy*, Descartes's last and most mature metaphysical work, he says: "I take the word *to think* to mean everything that happens within us such that we immediately perceive it ourselves." So I was not the one who invented the observation of the last lesson, here repeated, that *consciousness*, for the modern era, means "the immediate," the reality supposed to be self-immediate. But we have seen that there is no such "immediacy of thought to itself;" that, when I see the horse, *it* is what I see; I do not also see *my seeing*.

In order to describe this first act of seeing, one must perform a second mental act, which, when the first act is finished, will serve to recall or reproduce the first one. This new thought—the reflexive one—could be called "a thought about a thought"; but of course this new thought that thinks—or recalls—the former is no closer to the first, the *actual seeing*, than the latter was to the *seen reality*. Therefore, there is no question of "immediacy." This is why I maintain that a reality that consists in being self-immediate does not exist. This means we must ban the term *cogitatio* or consciousness from philosophy. What a scandal! How incredible! Still, it is what I hold. I want that clear.

Descartes's arguments will always be valid against a thesis like the classical one, which says that being, reality, is what is independent of me. But it is not valid if we take being, reality, to mean things being to me what they are and also my being among them.

Now; I do not expect even those heroes who were here last time to find me very clear if I change the most venerable terms of philosophy—being, reality—so that they mean being-to-me-what-they-are. And those heroes—you yourselves—would be absolutely right (any human activity can be carried to the point of heroism, and I would certainly call any audience that heard a second or a third lecture "heroes of listening").

To continue; the expressions I used—such as "the flower is a flower to me," or "the horse is a horse to me," and so forth—are, I feel, exact as preliminary expressions; and we have not seen the last of them. But they were never meant to be the last word in definitions. Quite the contrary, the breadth of the philosophical reform implied by what I have just said is clearly revealed in the way it forces us to revise nearly all the concepts of traditional philosophy, including the principal one: *being*, or *reality*. For just as these concepts were coined on the model of what for the Greeks and the Scholastics was the prototypical fact or phenomenon, the *res*, the substantial thing, that is, *this* horse, *this* man, so too the new conceptions of *being* and *reality*, the new meanings they now have, can only be clarified once we have seen the new phenomonon, the new fact that our analysis has found to be the most fundamental reality.

I have named it but it has yet to appear. I spoke of it the other day. We have not yet seen it because it is so close that we are not accustomed to seeing it. In the same way that the eye never sees the air that touches its cornea. Soon now we will lay eyes on it, in the course of a brief account of the two points that remain in my critique of Descartes and idealism generally. Let us turn to the third point.

Third point. In Descartes's judgment, when he doubts the world's reality, the world is abolished and only his *I* and his *doubt* remain. But we have observed that every act of awareness of being, every thought about what is real—except in the case of mere fantasy—puts us in direct contact with things. The *cogitatio, consciousness,* is, therefore, just the opposite of what Descartes imagined. It is essentially *transcendence;* it is precisely the *presence* of reality.

This thesis roundly contradicts the whole modern era and is, in its disguised technicality, the beginning of a brand new era. Some will say—naturally—that this is mere hairsplitting. But there is this difference between philosophers and barbers: both cut hair, but the philosopher also splits it.

However, what we must now notice is that, just as in the act called *seeing,* in the act termed "seeing a horse," the *horse* is present and is *reality* for me, so, when I doubt the world's reality, the world is far from abolished. Contrary to Descartes's opinion, when Descartes doubts the world, it remains there, all around him. Granted it no longer consisted of ocean and sky, of matter and form—as Scholasticism wanted him to believe—since he had doubted all its qualities. Yet, nevertheless, when I doubt the world, it remains there, outside me, distinct; at least what was doubted remains in the form of doubt.

To the old ontology, conceived in the framework of substantial things, it would have been unimaginable, it would have seemed a joke, to hold that the substance of reality could be *what is doubtful*. Nevertheless, as we shall see, this is the case.

What I am proposing when I say that the flower is the flower to me and the horse is the horse will be somewhat clearer if you give the verb *to be* an active, operational inflection; and, even better, something like that half voice that our languages have unfortunately lost; or, best of all, what recent grammarians call a "reciprocal half voice." For example, the Latin verb *luctare* does not just mean *to fight*, but "to fight each other," "to fight among themselves." But our language, forged under the aegis of a primitive philosophy, has no word to express a *being*, a *reality* in general, understood as accomplishment, as performance, as pure present or activity; and it has very few ways to express this in particular, in spite of the enormous role that active and reflexive verbs play in the Indo-European languages.

Thus; the *flower's-being-a-flower* to me can be analyzed into having its scent smelt by me, coloring me with its color, caressing me with its fleshy petals, which are both silky and clinging. This is the flower *being a flower to me*. This state of affairs, and countless others that, in order to be designated together, would require a general verb that meant the equivalent of "the flower enflowers me," or something just as extravagant.

Now, just as the flower smells, colors, and flowers me, so, in the same way, when I put the world in doubt, the world continues there, weighing on me and weighing on Descartes—although he refuses to admit it—for in spite of its having lost all other qualities, it continues to oppress us and sting us with one sole troublesome quality: its very doubtfulness. Or, to invent a terrible-sounding word that would have delighted the Scholastics—so clever at naming things, but especially at picking ugly names—a word fully worthy of having been spoken for the first time in the four-teenth century by a gargoyle of Notre Dame, we could say that when I doubt the world's reality, what remains abso-lutely real is me doubting and the world "doubtifying" me, injecting me with its doubtfulness, as oil pours into a car. Or, if you prefer, we can use instead a very Argentinian expression, even though it is a little too common. We could say that when I doubt, there is an I who doubts and the world "pestering" me.

Ladies and gentlemen, I take this occasion to point out something peculiar to philosophy. We deal now with the most abstract and abstruse facet of the entire edifice of phi-losophy. This abstractness is increased with the announce-ment of my new perspective, which is more difficult than the traditional ones: the perspectives of antiquity and the modern era. Still, without any intermediary arguments, you will perceive the concrete meaning of what I have just said if you will only attend to what the other half of the world—the human half—is "being-to-you" at this moment.

Tell me how we should characterize that part of the human world that is now before you—that is, the political and social part of it—if not by saying that it is *something* you are doubt-ful about, that oppresses you with its doubtfulness, that *doubtifies* and *pesters* you. It turns out that the most abstract word is the most adequate name to describe what is most concrete.

And if you are familiar enough with contemporary phys-ics you will know that for the physicist, too, matter has evaporated. Max Planck, the great man who reformed phys-ical science with his discovery of *quanta*, said—long ago—that the only quality left to matter was space, its spatiality; the existence of "quanta" means that at a given instant it is impossible to find where an electron is in space. In other words, we have an emptiness, an absence of matter, pure spatiality. That is, the physicist's matter has been demater-ialized, and all that is left is his doubt regarding matter.

Although we cannot trust everyday language, it undoubtedly yields remarkable insights, especially about human affairs. As it happens, your situation vis-à-vis the social and political world, which is the same as the physicist's vis-à-vis matter, is neatly described in everyday language when we say man is "in a sea of doubt." Each word in this familiar, idiomatic Spanish phrase is marvellously apt—even "sea," which appears to be a vague metaphor.

As we said on the first day, while *we have ideas*, we *inhabit* beliefs. Now, while one who inhabits *this* or *that* belief is securely at home in it, this is not the case when one is "in" doubt. Doubt, belief's ugly sister, is also something that one is "in." But "being in doubt" is precisely to be not on *solid*, but on treacherous, ground; it is a way of *being* that causes vertigo; we are overwhelmed by doubt. Doubt, then, is a fluid, watery element, like the ocean when you are out of your depth. To doubt is to sink, a despairing submersion almost like drowning. Notice, by the way, that in this new philosophy the most ordinary words acquire the status of technical terms. Indirectly this demonstrates that our new philosophy is no mere extension of the old one, but a new beginning. Because in Ionia and Greece with the birth of the first philosophy, thinkers had the same experience. In order to express the new realities they had discovered or glimpsed, Heraclitus and Parmenides, Plato and Aristotle, were obliged to use commonplace metaphors from the everyday language of the taverns. Today, these old alehouse metaphors reach us with the status, the asepsis and the hieratic mien of words that have achieved the solemnity of terminology. Country philosophers should take heed of this fact.

Fourth point. In spite of Descartes's discovery in doubting of just what he hoped to find, that is, something he could *not* doubt—a first certainty, a first principle, a primary reality—he paid it little attention. He merely glanced at it for a moment, and with disdain. Descartes was extremely disdainful; one only has to look at the eyes in the extraordinary portrait by Frans Hals, the only great portrait we have of a great philosopher.

All that interests Descartes about this doubt is what it has in common with *seeing, hearing, dreaming, reasoning*, with all *thinking*, or *cogitatio*. That is, he is only interested in its supposedly immediate reality. Yet if he had only paid closer attention, he would have noticed—had he reflected on what happened to him when he doubted—that the latter, his doubt, did not begin by itself. His reasoning was an integral part of his doubting; his previous reasoning was an integral part of his present doubt, inasmuch as it gave rise to it. And it was also part of its meaning. Without the reasoning, the doubt would not exist, would make not sense. Therefore, if we admit the reality of this prior doubt, the methodical doubt, we must also acknowledge the reality of the prior reasoning that is continued, and exists, in essential connection with that doubt.

This is obvious. But, in addition, the reasoning that gave rise to the doubt did not just appear either. This reasoning came about, was entertained, and has the meaning it has because at an earlier point Descartes *decided to* think about fundamental reality, decided to go in search of a first, indubitable reality: in short, because Descartes decided to philosophize. The reasonings that produced this doubt came from that decision; and that decision and those reasonings are active in this doubt. So that if one tries to subtract all this from the fact of doubting, the latter has no meaning, is not what it is, and, therefore, is nonexistent.

But this *active* decision is by no means theoretical, but an act of will. Descartes resolved to do philosophy because apparently he needed to do something to exist, to subsist, and because that *something* was "theorizing."

Thus we see that behind all theory there is a previous decision to theorize. And from that decision, and qualified by it—so that without the decision they would be meaningless—flow all the strategies of reason the doubt provoked. So, with the same radical certainty that he asserted the existence of his doubt, Descartes could assert, and should have, the prior existence of his theory and of his pre-theoretical decision to "theorize." Or, to put it differently, theory is not born spontaneously in men but results from a previously made decision to theorize.

Prior to the man who doubts methodically, then—who theorizes—is the man who has yet to theorize but who decides, for one reason or another, to do so. Yet this decision, in turn, came about and was nourished by the fact that, earlier, Descartes had at some point found he was surrounded by things without knowing what to do with them, since every learned or received view about his natural and social world, the world of things, seemed wrong, uncertain, and unsupported by proof.

Therefore, behind and prior to any methodical and theoretical doubt, yet forming an integral part of it, ultimately giving it what truth it has, stands Descartes the man, who exists in a milieu that he fails to understand, in shadows and darkness, with no one to turn to since no one else can explain things. He is thus completely alone and obliged to do *something* to subsist, to mobilize himself vis-à-vis things and to affirm himself in their regard: that is, obliged to govern his own conduct. If we refuse to recognize this entire process as reality, as real, we can no more admit the reality of that first doubt, which, as we now see, was neither first nor even authentic, but fictitious and secondary. Fictitious doubt, because *methodical*, is as its name suggests, only the thought that one is in doubt, or it is the idea—the theory—that one must doubt everything that is not self-evident. The all too real doubt is the other, pre-philosophical one that led Descartes to doubt in the first place. That doubt was not theory, not thinking one should doubt, but total, real, and operative *(ejecutivo)* doubt.

Notice the new meaning that an old, informal, and even

awkward Latin aphorism acquires: *Primum vivere; deinde philosophari*. In truth, living does come first, and *philosophizing, theorizing*, comes after. But this *after* is neither solely nor even particularly a matter of chronology. The *deinde*, the *next*, is a *query*, implying a causal relation; for we saw that Descartes turned to philosophy when he was perplexed and because he didn't know what to do in order to survive—when he had no choice but to acquire clear and distinct ideas regarding reality. In short, one cannot live without philosophizing and, more generally, without theorizing, gaining an orientation with respect to this element we unthinkingly and improperly call "the world in which we exist," or "the world in which we live."

So that the true meaning of the clumsy old Latin saying is "we philosophize because we live." Theory begins, and has its essential root, in life. *Theory* is life; but, at the same time, one cannot live without theorizing. It is just as Socrates said to his judges, the mass-men of Athens, two thousand years ago: "A life without theory is not a liveable life." *Life*, without some kind of a philosophy, is not liveable. This is not how it should be; it is the way it is. And anyone who fails to recognize this fact is simply unaware of the awkward, roughhewn, wayward philosophy that supports him and gives him his orientation, that cloaks him like the dust cloud that, golden in the setting sun, follows a tiny band of horsemen across the Pampas.

Observe that to catch Descartes out, we only had to take him at his word, seriously confront his fundamental thesis—according to which "I doubt, therefore I am" is the first truth—and then look more closely at the specific contents of this doubt; in this way we found that Descartes's thesis was self-contradictory because unwittingly it contained the following additional series of prior theses, all more fundamental than his first thesis, and all unwittingly overlooked:

(1) In order for man to doubt and theorize, he must already exist.

(2) This prior existence, since it both makes possible and motivates his doubt, is true, primary, radical existence, the fundamental reality of living and not of doubting or thinking.

(3) Man's existence, prior to his theorizing, is real existence. (Notice that I use the word *existence* in its most traditional sense and not in the one it acquired a short time ago in the recently named "existential philosophy," which is nothing but the latest of four attempts to base philosophy on the new idea of life, on the great idea of life that, willy-nilly, will be the sole basis for the next era of mankind. Yes, 'four attempts,' of which Dilthey's, eighty years ago, was the first, the most inspired, the initiation; but, unfortunately, its expression was so inadequate that, for reasons I explained years ago in "Wilhelm Dilthey and the Idea of Life,"* it availed nothing, and some of us have subsequently had to rediscover it for ourselves. The second attempt—speaking chronologically, but the most inadequate in its published formulation—was my own, as I gave it out in university courses and in two or three brief publications in England and Germany. The third attempt, by Jaspers, a psychiatrist and doctor who made an untimely switch to philosophy, offered a reinterpretation with certain insights but was flawed because of the author's lack of philosophical expertise. And the fourth attempt is the one by Heidegger; his is undoubtedly admirable, but in its first installment it showed itself to be palsied and somewhat paralyzed. Now, as I was saying, man's existence prior to his theorizing, his real existence, consists in his discovering that he has to subsist in an element that surrounds and imprisons him; in an obscure and confusing element that is an enigma, and with regard to which he has no notion as to how to conduct himself. That element could be called—improperly—the "world." Ever since my first book, *Meditations on*

*Ortega, *Concord and Liberty*, Helene Weyl, Translator (New York: W.W. Norton, 1946), pp. 129–82.

Quixote, 1914, I have referred to this element as "circum-stances." At another time we shall see why.)

(4) Still prior to any *Cogito ergo sum:* this having, perforce, at every moment to do with specific circumstances is what is usually called "life." Therefore, human life, the life of each one of us, is the fundamental reality in which all other realities arise or make their appearance. *To live,* then, means always finding oneself immersed in specific circumstances and having to do something to keep one's head above water.

(5) Because man's circumstances are always and ulti-mately enigmatic, obscure, and confused, man does not really know what to do in order to subsist among them. And to a greater or lesser degree, he is always lost or in danger of losing his way. What should we do then? When we don't know what to do with our surroundings, the only thing left is to think about those surroundings, solve their enigma, and, according to what we find, design a program of things to be done—an occupational life-plan. Thus, when man doesn't know what to do, all he can do is attempt *to know.* This lies at the root of the theorizing of science and philos-ophy and, generally, of what is called "truth" and "reason." *Reason,* at its most authentic, is vital reason. This means, strictly and concretely, that the intellect, or pure reason alone, does not create basic concepts, but is driven to them by vital necessity. Or, as I wrote in *The Vital Theme* in 1923, pure reason is circumscribed by vital reason. Lost in his circum-stances and obliged to do something in order to subsist, man needs a meaning for what he does, needs it to be the appro-priate thing. It would not matter in the least to someone immortal if a mistake were made, because it could always be corrected the following day. But mortal man needs—willy-nilly—to be right the first time. His life depends on it. He has to do everything possible to make certain he is right, and that what he does is true.

(6) (Last thesis): All the above can be summarized as fol-

lows: any thesis that was ever proposed, or ever could be proposed, as the first thesis of philosophy, already *presupposes* life as the fundamental reality, within which, and in view of which, that thesis arose. Therefore, the really fundamental thesis asserts both that life—wherein all other theses arise—is the primordial reality and that the principles of the theory of reason are not rational but simply the exigencies of our lives.

Descartes's mind worked so prodigiously well that it did so even against his wishes. The proof of this is that his *Discourse on Method*, with which his philosophy begins, is three-quarters biography. This fact is surprising, but until now it has remained grotesquely unexplained. For, although it seems impossible, and must surely be the scandal of Western philosophy, the *Discourse* has yet to be understood. There are several commentaries on it—not many, really, considering it is the life-plan of the entire modern era. There are many scandals in the "life and culture of world thought." Long ago I decided that whenever I came across one of them in the course of my work, I would point it out. This is one of them. There are several commentaries. There is even an extraordinarily erudite one that, as far as erudition is concerned, leaves nothing to be desired: by Etienne Gilson. Gilson is a perfectly respectable intellect—I have the greatest respect for him—who has a firm grasp of certain aspects of medieval philosophy; and what he knows, he knows well and conveys clearly and with precision. But I must say that, while I have learned several unimportant things from reading him, as a philosopher he is a nullity. As a philosophical mind he is kindergartenish, naïve, and Adam-like. In all his lengthy commentary on the *Discourse* there is not the slightest hint of the nature of the book called *Discourse on Method*, a book that, by the way, is a prologue.

What Descartes considers his formal philosophical doctrine only begins about halfway through the book; everything before that is a memoir. But, as one would expect—in the case of a mind of the caliber of Descartes's—this memoir, far from being chatter or inessential tales, turns out to be the essential biography of every intellectual and, generally, of Everyman.

"Since I could find no one—says Descartes—whose opinion seemed to me preferable to anyone else's, I was obliged to be my own guide. *Mais, comme un homme qui marche seul et dans les tenebres . . .*" (But, as one who travels alone and in darkness . . .)—that is, everyone—"I resolved to go slowly . . . and find a method for gaining a knowledge of all the things my mind was capable of knowing."

As you have just seen, we had only to turn the private memoirs of this man into theoretical theses for the whole first part of the *Discourse on Method* to become the philosophy of the future. In other words, out of the ashes of intellectualist and idealist Cartesian philosophy, of the Cartesianism of *Cogito ergo sum*, the "I think, therefore I am," out of that false Cartesianism and its ashes, like the immortal phoenix, a Cartesianism of life is born, and one of its fundamental theses goes like this: "I am, therefore I think."

Earlier I said that my critique would culminate in an homage. Let us say, with the Provost of Paris: Descartes is dead and with him the modern era. Long live Descartes and with him the future!

On the first day, when I outlined the program for these four lectures, I made clear my intention of stating, in brief formulas, the overall architecture of my philosophical doctrine—in such a way that it would all converge gradually on its special theme, which I call "historical reason." Later I saw there was no alternative but to pause at length and examine the first thesis of philosophy. This much we have already done; but now I must take the bit in my teeth and, as promised, set off to cover what follows from this initial thesis, until we reach the point where my notion of historical reason emerges. Although the latter is only the index to an entire philosophy, I hope that even so it will be sufficiently clear and precise.

We began with what is usually called—what each one calls—in sorrow and joy, in anguish and hopefulness, *one's life*. This is the fundamental reality. It is what we discover to be already there, not in a more or less theoretical, hypothetical way, not as mere supposition, but as what is always there, before any theory; that is, qua *being*, as what *is real*.

Now we must discover what "all this" really is—discover the consistency of what exists. According to traditional terminology, we call *what* something is, its "essence." However, since *all that there is* not only exists, but consists of this or that, I prefer the term "consistency." Whereby the old pair of Scholastic terms, "existence" and "essence" is replaced by the following one, which to my mind is more sprightly and exact: "existence" and "consistency."

We state that, based on all the evidence, life is what exists, and we propose it as the prototype of existence—just as for antiquity "the world" was the prototype of existence, and as "thought," consciousness, mind, was the primordial reality for the modern era.

But now we must ascertain the consistency of this life. And since the new reality we discovered was *something* hidden behind the world that thinking thought, and even behind the thinking that thought that world, and since, in consequence, it is a reality prior to all this, an even purer reality, we must make every effort not to employ concepts, in describing or thinking about this reality, that were formulated to think the world and thought—because now we know that the latter notions are secondary, derivative concepts.

What we need, then, is an entirely new philosophy, a whole new repertoire of fundamental—indigenous—concepts. We stand in the presence of a new source of illumination. But it cannot be won too abruptly, because then you and I would not understand one another. We have to take off gradually—as pilots say—from traditional philosophy, from the repertoire of received, familiar, and commonplace concepts; in the meantime we must use those concepts that come closest, that approximate the new reality we have glimpsed.

And so I will begin by saying that life—each person's life is our focus—in contrast to all other known or supposed realities, is purely and exclusively "occurrence." Living happens to me. In its turn, life is made up of countless events. (And people say philosophy is so difficult. The definition of life I have just given could have been said in a bar, over drinks, in chatting with a friend.) *Life* is what happens to me. An expression like that might well be the first words of a tango. (By the way, some day we shall have to speak at length about the words of the tango; there is a subject about which, I dare say, much remains to be said.) *Life* occurs; it happens-to-me. And our lives are, simply, that first *this* happens and then *that* happens. Now we must attempt an adequate conceptualization of just what this something is that is mere happening—that is, occurrence. The problem—and here the tango fails us—is that this something must be understood in a radical way, which is what makes this *philosophy*. Philosophy is intellectual—radicalism. Because what confronts us is not my being something or, rather, two things: body and soul; or that this thing that I am should be here, among other things, within a large thing called the world—provisionally, the earth—or that here one thing or another happens to me. No! Not at all! There *is* nothing but this *happening-to-me*. There is nothing that is not *pure occurrence*. Which means that *living* is not my body and soul here on this earth; because *body*, *soul*, and *earth* are not radical realities but ideas we have had, while *living*, about the nature of the reality that I am and that I inhabit. These ideas may be radical formulations that are original with me, or I may have taken them from my social milieu. That is, perhaps they were first formulated by someone else in another era. The issue that arises at this juncture was treated—I believe with a certain exactness—in my essay "Ideas and Beliefs," to which I said we would have to refer more than once. Here is part of that essay:

If we are asked what we really walk on, we answer at once that it is the Earth. By this we understand a star of a certain size and constitution, that is, a mass of cosmic matter revolving around the sun with sufficient regularity and precision so that we can count on it. This is our firm belief, and this is why for us it is reality; and because it is reality for us, we automatically count on it, we never question it in our daily lives. But the truth is that if the same question had been asked a man living in the seventh century B.C., his answer would have been quite different. How did he view the earth? It was a goddess, the mother goddess, Demeter. Not a mass of matter but a divine power with its own desires and caprices. This should suffice to warn us that the primary, authentic reality of earth is neither of these things, that the star Earth and the goddess Earth are not reality, pure and simple, but two ideas—or perhaps one true idea and one false idea about that reality, two ideas formulated by specific individuals on a given day with great effort. This means that the reality the earth is for us did not simply originate when the Earth did, that the latter is not "that" by itself; instead, we owe this name to some man, to many earlier men; and besides, its truth is the result of many difficult decisions. In short, this truth is problematic and open to question; therefore, the Earth as star and the Earth as goddess are two theories, two interpretations.

The same point could be made regarding everything, which leads us to the discovery that the reality in which we believe we live, on which we count, and which serves as ultimate reference for all our hopes and fears, is the work and creation of other men and not primary, authentic reality. *In order to encounter authentic reality in its sheer nakedness we would have to remove all the layers of today's and yesterday's beliefs, all those theories that are nothing but interpretations thought up by man about what he finds, in living, in himself, and in his milieu.* Prior to all interpretation, the Earth was not even a *thing*, because thing is itself a configuration of being, an idea that defines the peculiar way something has of behaving (as distinct, say, from the behavior of a phantom), an idea the mind thought up to explain to itself that primary reality.

If we were properly grateful, we would have realized that what the Earth has been to us—that is, a *star* or, formerly, a *goddess*—and what, as theories, as ideas, helped us know how to behave in their regard and let us be at ease and not live in perpetual fear, all this we owe to the efforts and intelligence of others. Without their intercession we would have the same relationship to the Earth and all around us as did the first men on Earth; that is, we would live in constant fear. We have inherited all their efforts in the form of beliefs, and this is the capital on which we live. The monumental and, at the same time, the essential, elementary discovery the West will make in the coming years, when it recovers from the drunken spell of folly that began in the eighteenth century—and which it is in the process now of regurgitating—is that man is above all an inheritor. And it is this rather than anything else that distinguishes him from the animals. But awareness of being an inheritor means being historically aware. Our lack of a historical awareness that man owes everything to his past is just like the ingratitude of the arrow of which I spoke the other day.

The authentic reality of the earth has no configuration at all, no mode of being; it is pure enigma. Taken thus, in its primary, naked consistency, the earth is only the ground that for the moment supports us without the least assurance it will not give way the next second; it is what allowed us to escape some danger, but also what, as distance, separates us from a beloved or from our children; it is what sometimes faces us with the bothersome character of being uphill and sometimes with the delightful condition of being downhill. The Earth in itself, stripped of the ideas man has formed about it, is not, then, anything at all, but merely an uncertain repertoire of facilities and difficulties that affect our life.

The oldest interpretation of what the Earth is can be gleaned from the Latin etymology of the word. *Terra* apparently derives from *tersa*, which means dry, that is, *solid ground*, offering a good footing. In this primitive interpretation of the Earth, the latter is defined—as you see—according to what it does for us, as distinct from what happens in its watery alternative. It is in this sense that authentic, primary reality has no configuration in and of itself. This is why it cannot be called 'world.' It is an enigma posed to our existence. To live is to be irrevocably immersed in the enigmatic. Man reacts to this primordial, pre-intellectual enigma by activating his intellectual faculties, above all, his imagination. He creates a mathematical world, a physical world, a religious, a moral, a political, and a poetic world, which are all effectively worlds because they each have a configuration and offer a plan, an order. These imaginary worlds are set alongside the enigma of authentic reality, and when they seem a close enough approximation they are accepted. But, of course, they are never confused with reality itself.*

*In culling these paragraphs from *Ideas and Beliefs*, for presentation in the classroom, Ortega made a few brief additions to the original text. [Ed.]

4

The need for concepts not created for thinking
either the world or thought. The failure of traditional concepts to engage present problems. This
is the true source of our disorientation. Review
of our itinerary. Life is uncertainty. God and
man's condition. Paradise and circumstances.
The circumstances comprise facilities and obstacles. What is the 'I'? It is futurization, a program
for being circumstantially. A series of discoveries. First: Man is the existence of a non-existence; he is indigent being. Second. Man is the
attempt to realize his program in the midst of his
circumstances; his relative inadaptation makes
him unhappy. Third: Acceptance of life makes
the risk envolved an enterprise.

As WE SAW the other day, in order to exist man always has
to be doing something. But, of all his countless tasks, the
one he engages in most often and most insistently is "wish
ful thinking."

I am not certain—since in this regard man is persistent
and indefatigable—if "wishful thinking" is not the way to
classify my feeling that despite their theoretical abstruse-
ness, their diabolical abstraction, my lectures have actually
caught your interest a bit. This is certainly to your credit.

Grateful for your effort of attention, then, I have decided to reciprocate by adding one more lecture. This way I will gain a little more time, the lack of which has been more distressing to me than you can imagine; because I have always had before me the specter of how little time there was at my disposal, and it has seemed to me that with each unnecessary word I was murdering one of those invaluable minutes. This is why I asked the dean of the Faculty to allow me one more lecture. With his customary benevolence he has acceded to my wish.

Without expressly saying so and as though in passing, we have given a quintessential history of philosophy, so as to show the two great theses that have nourished Western thought for two thousand years like two highly concentrated vitamin pills: the ancient thesis that holds that "the world of things" is the primordial reality, and the modern thesis that, as a result of Descartes's critique of the former thesis, holds thought to be the most solid reality of all.

In turn we criticized this modern thesis, energetically reworking the analysis from which it came; and we discovered that, beneath the world that thinking thinks, and even beneath the thinking of that world, is the "human life" of each of us, a reality purer than, and prior to, either; this human life motivates, and is therefore prior to, all theory; it is the ontological ambience or region of reality in which all theses—I stress: any and all theses—must arise.

Now then, I concluded, everything depends on our managing to find concepts with which to think this new ante-world and ante-thought reality—concepts that are other than those invented to think the world and to think thought, because from our new perspective the old concepts are mediated, secondary, and derivative. This is why I cannot define the reality of my life by saying it consists in my being— that is, in my body and soul being—on Earth; because *body*, *soul*, and *Earth* are nothing but interpretations, theories, that living man invents to explain the reality in which he exists and is.

As an example, I referred to the belief that the earth is a star, as opposed to the belief the ancients held that the Earth was a goddess. Star-Earth and goddess-Earth are simply two theories evolved by man to understand or try to understand what this thing *Earth* is, which, in its naked, purest reality is simply what supports us, what sometimes quakes and frightens us, what separates us from our beloved, our children, what allows us to run away when we need to, what is hard going uphill, and easy going downhill. The Earth is first and foremost what happens to us where *it* is directly concerned.

And in like manner with the *horse* and the *flower* we repeatedly used as examples in the second lecture. (So repetitious was I that Ramón Gómez de la Serna, obliged as he was—he, a poet, and a brilliant one—out of friendship to attend a philosophy lecture, said to me when it was over that I had had so many horses charging past that the audience began to bet on them.) *Earth, horse*, or *flower* are not things that are primordially there, but things that happened to us. Therefore, they are not things; because *thing* is a utopian notion about something that *is* in itself, that has a *fixed being*, permanent, given. Just as the *horse* and the *flower*, before being construed by the imagination—that is, theorized into things—are only "what happens to us with the *horse*" and "what happens to us with the *flower*."

To the Greeks, *being* meant *stable reality*, given once and for all, permanent. Beginning with Parmenides, the Greeks used *being* to denote unchanging quietude. The precise term the Greeks used for this peculiar aspect of the real was *ousia*, substance. Substance is what is ultimately self-identical, ontological quietude. This is why it is of no use for thinking about the reality of our life. Let us topple the concept "sub-stance" from its millennial throne. It is useless as a funda-mental category of reality, as *kyrios on*.

This doesn't mean that we cannot use the concept *sub-stance* for relatively menial tasks. But what consists in *hap-pening* and *occurring* is pure flux and movement. Life is essentially, magnificently, *dis*quietude!

Ser (being), our Spanish word, comes—as you know—from *sedere:* to be seated. That's how much "quietude" it implies! But life is never remaining seated, it has no unchanging being, given once and for all; instead, it is con-stantly happening and occurring. Life is constantly be-ing and un-being; it is always coming to be and ceasing to be at the same time. One should never say that life *is*, but rather that it *lives*.

We must retire all the terms I was forced to use in the previous lectures to lead you, little by little, from your for-mer intellectual orientation to our new perspective.

It is no longer apposite to say that things *are to me*, or that living is man *being* or *existing* in the world; because there is neither *world*, nor *man*, in the sense of *body* and *soul*, nor is there even being in the sense of self-identical being, given and fixed once and for all.

It is curious that the only formulas, the only terms, we can retain are the old ones, the very first in the history of my thought. That is, that, ultimately and truly, there is the coexistence of *I* with what is *not-I*, as I said here, in Buenos Aires in 1916; or, that the *fundamental reality is I and my circumstances*—as I said in *Meditations on Quixote* in 1914.

For it is no more correct to say that I am just there. I happen to *myself*. In life I constantly have to do with what I call *I* and which gives me a great deal to do. I am not my body; I am not my soul. Because *body* and *soul*—as I said—are only theoretical hypotheses, rather clumsy and confused ones at that.

Science has come to a dead end as far as the concepts *body* and *soul* are concerned. Today *body* has no clear meaning either in the sense of material body, or in the sense of a biological one. As far as *soul* is concerned, in terms of theory, of science, it is little more than a word. . . .

Once again we have lost our way. We have lost our way with respect to those two realities X and X' that we call *body* and *soul* and are so important to us. You will understand that if we are lost with respect to such fundamental themes, we are unlikely to be much better off regarding others that are far less important (politics, for example) but that nevertheless would serve to illuminate our basic concepts, and many other things that are implicated therein.

Or do you believe that what is happening today, that terrible absorption of man by politics has come about really, truly, and finally only because he doesn't know *what to do* with his institutions?

Because it is obvious—there is no doubt about it—that what is happening in the world today on the political level, which is always and in essence a superficial level (and to believe otherwise is not to have given five minutes of serious thought to the difference between good and bad politics, or even to what politics itself is); what is happening is that no one has any idea what to do with our institutions. This "no idea what to do" is sometimes disguised as its opposite: *because* there is "no idea what to do," an exaggerated, frenetic busyness ensues. This false "having a great deal to do," which hides the inanity of its content behind a superlative gesture, is an "extreme doing," or "extremism." Extremism has always appeared in history when no one knows what to do.

Yet the fact is that with or without superlative disguises, the situation is everywhere the same. The process is further advanced in some countries than in others, but everywhere it is substantially the same. When you question those in favor of the most radical solution, when you button-hole them and point out the weakness of their institutional projects, they are forced to admit—in this they are sincere, authentic, serious—that the latter were adopted because the old projects were discredited. And they are so right! In countries where the old ways are retained for the sake of continuity, one suspects an additional reason is that the new ways seem less than viable. And again these people are quite right!

Since everybody today is wrong, this results, as I said to the Friends of Art Circle last spring, in everyone ending up being right, except that one man's right is another's wrong. Each does what he does precisely because he doesn't know what *to* do, because political life, artistic life, has ceased to be authentic and has become, pro tem, essentially inauthentic, as has happened before in history. But on the subject of the authenticity and inauthenticity of life, which dates from the beginning of my philosophy, I can say no more here; time will not allow it; it is lock-stepping me along like a criminal. Of course it has been amply demonstrated that the only way to combat a lack of clarity in secondary areas of life, such as politics, is by doing as man has always done in times of crisis, that is, by making life authentic again, by reconstructing its foundations—by beginning all over again to clarify fundamental themes, by adjusting and updating our basic repertoire of ideas so it accords with the present level of our historical experience, in short, by an intellectual rebirth. With man, who is always an inheritor and who has always a past, every historical birth is a renaissance.

This loss of direction in political matters indicates how much we suffer from something even more serious: it is not in politics that we have lost our way; our disorientation here is merely a symptom of a crisis in man's beliefs, and, moreover, of a crisis in his beliefs about himself.

You will understand that since I feel as I do, whenever someone tells me, the way people do nowadays, that he disagrees with me in politics, instead of concurring I give the same preemptory reply I have been giving for fifteen or twenty years: "Just a minute. Don't expect me to disagree with you in politics. Where we differ is in our biology, our physics, our mathematics, our history, our psychology, our sociology, our ethics, our logic, and our philosophy. You, sir, are full of decrepit, gangrenous ideas about all these things. In this regard you have archaic opinions and grotesque notions. Imagine saying we differ in politics when that is only the most apparent consequence of this whole group of outmoded ideas! No, my friend! We could never disagree about politics, because long before we got to that subject we'd have stopped speaking to one another."

What has just been said must not be taken as a detour from the direction of these lectures, which as you remember was the following: I began by saying I would speak about what was happening in the world today—the world, of course, that interests this Faculty of Philosophy—and that I would deal with the essence of my subject. And, I hastened to add, what essentially happens today is that once again man has lost his way.

The first concrete example of this disorientation is that the notion of man himself, according to which he is both body and soul, has become problematic and we don't know what to do about it. For this reason, since in speaking of what is happening we usually refer to the obvious, and since the obvious is by definition what is on the surface, and since the surface of history is politics, I was obliged to point out that our disorientation in politics was merely the most recent consequence of the crisis of beliefs to which I referred earlier. It seems to me, then, that the design of my lectures could not be more coherent.

Now man never emerges from one of these historical crises without a *renovatio*, a *restaurare*, a *renascentia*, a *renaissance*—call it what you will. The latter consists in general in a fun-

damental innovation of the entire repertoire of man's opinions about himself and the world, by adjusting and updating
the system of concepts and ideas that man has about reality—that is, about himself and the universe—to accord with
his present historical experience. We found that human life,
the life of each of us, was a fundamental reality on which
we could absolutely depend; and we spoke of it first in the
most abstract of terms, saying something about it that was
totally removed from the philosophical tradition: that is, that
it consisted in *my* coexistence with *things*, the *mutual and
reciprocal existing* of man and world.

Then we refined our understanding of this reality, saying
that this coexistence, or mutual existence, this reiprocal being
(*serse*) on the part of man and world, was not a *thing* but
rather an event, to such a fundamental extent that we could
not admit as part of the reality of life anything quiet or static
in nature.

I am not a thing—as I repeat. I am not *my body;* I am not
my soul. The *soul* is an extremely confused idea we have from
Aristotle, *something* supposed to exist in a manner distinct
from our bodies but retaining many of their characteristics.

From our point of view Aristotle's famous spiritualism is
a legacy of materialism. This *soul*-thing that is meant to be
different from a *body*-thing (which was the prototype—we
have often said in these lectures—for the formation of the
concepts of *being* and *thing*) can only be a *quasi-thing.* By
comparison with a reality that is pure event, the *being of a
soul* is *quasi-being;* it is material being—more diaphanous, it
is true, but matter nevertheless—for ponderous reasons I
will examine in the next lecture.

To find a useful concept in Aristotle that is adequate to
the reality of our life, we must turn to what he considered
the exclusive property of God: pure *enérgeia*, pure act or
activity, absolute agility. Of course my life is not meant to
replace God or to be divine. On the contrary it is human,

all too human, the humanity of the human; it is to have wonderful and adverse things happening to me, to always have to be doing something so that wonderful and adverse things will *keep* happening *to me* and I can avoid—strange, profound paradox—one of the two things that can never happen in my life: *my death*. This is why I do what I do: to keep from dying. And this *dying* is one of the two things that can never happen in my life. My death will exist for those who survive me, but it doesn't happen to me, it doesn't exist for me. I am not present at my death. And the same is true of my birth. When I become aware of living—curiously enough—I have already been born. My birth is only a story others tell me. It is a tale I am told. My death isn't even that: no one can relate it to me. Thus it is only an idea, a theory, albeit the most serious and tremendous theory of all. Being born and dying are the only two things that aren't part of my life—where everything is possible: fortune and misfortune, happiness and unhappiness. Or to put it another way, the astounding reality that is my life—without being infinite—has neither a beginning nor an end as part of it. It would be infinite if the absolute certainty of being immortal were a part of my life; but immortality is only, and at most, a *belief* and an *idea*. On the other hand, the constant uncertainty over whether I will still be alive a moment from now is a part of my life. But my uncertainty about every next instant, every tomorrow, the future, is not fear of death itself. Otherwise, the hope for, or belief in, immortality—of whatever variety—would be impossible It is incorrect to say that man has entirely renounced immortality. The truth is that in principle man is equally open to immortality and to death. Although it has neither beginning nor end, my life is nevertheless not infinite, because as "fundamental event" it is "fundamental uncertainty"—as I said long ago in *Meditations on Quixote*. For this reason an elegant and exact motto for us all would be the one a Burgundian knight of the fifteenth century carried on his shield: *"Rien ne m'est sur que la chose incertaine"* ("I am only certain of uncertainty").

Life, then, is the encounter with something that, vaguely, and with no pretense to exact meaning, I call 'I' existing in circumstances, in an ever-problematic existence, without any certainty about my existing the next moment, yet forced, in order to secure my continued existence, always to be doing something in an element that is not this 'I.' This is why *life* is not solely 'I.' *I* am only one ingredient in my life; the other is *my circumstances.* One is just as real as the other. This is why I said we had gone beyond all idealism and all solipsism. According to the former thesis, since there is only *I* and my *thoughts,* "existence" is "living within the confines of the self." If life were only that! What more could one ask for? But that is not life's way of being real; on the contrary, it is God's way. For God there are no limits beyond himself. What is not God is nothing, or a *quasi-nothing;* that is, the world of matter and the world touched by matter.

Because it is so little known—even in Germany where it comes from—I will tell you about the fantastic yet unquestionably ingenious explanation of matter that came to one Franz von Baader, a Catholic-theosophist active in Munich around 1820—the prototype of the Romantic thinker. Baader had considerable influence on Schelling and a certain amount on Hegel, in spite of the fact that, or precisely because, Hegel spoke disparagingly of him. I shall translate his rather prolix views into my own more concise words: God, the omnipotent being, creates the angels and gives them plenitudinous being; however, the angels backslide; and God in his anger emits a decree of extinction, of annihilation, against them. The angels, which are plenitudinous being, are about to stop *being* altogether, are about to become non-being. But a moment too late—if "moments" make any sense in the context of eternity—God feels remorse over his first decree; a tide of compassion rises in his sacrosanct heart, and he dashes off a second decree canceling the first one. But this second decree arrives late. The first one has already begun to take effect. The angels, once plenary being, are now almost non-being, are by this time next to nothing. That minimum degree of being, that being as little as anything can be, being next to nothing, being almost nothing, is how he envisioned matter.

For God, then, there are no limits—we said—beyond himself. Beyond God there is only that "next to nothing" of a world, a world that he created. And a world created by someone is only the realization "out there" of a thought. But this "out there"—the mere externalization of a thought—is not really *out there*. Just as the world we dreamed of when we were adolescents was not genuinely *out there*: the world in which we were princes, and in which every girl's starry glance was directed at us. No! That didn't happen *out there!*

Hence we must say of God that his existence is solitary, that he is alone with his thoughts, with his inscrutable designs, that he lacks ambience, knows no real outside; instead he is alone, in his own element, in himself as element, floating in his own inwardness; that is, he has neither occupation nor preoccupation, self-absorbedly, perpetually, he weaves the mysterious fabric of his musings. God is the absolute meditator; he is the eternal dreamer inhabiting his own infinite dream.

Of course, as a philosopher and at this first stage of my philosophy, I don't know yet if this God exists. The God I spoke of is an idea I developed to serve as an exact model of a certain mode of being real, of the mode peculiar to a purported entity existing within itself, without surroundings, with nothing touching it, hurting it, contradicting it, or offering resistance to it. Such an entity has no difficulty existing.

This model is a contrastive example to show that man's condition is very different. For man, *to exist* means just what the etymology of the verb suggests: *existere, to stand outside oneself;* to perforce be in a foreign, negative, hostile element, where neither my ideas, nor my plans, nor my desires are automatically realized, that does not accept me or easily coincide with me. That element in which man must exist is his *circumstances.* If these circumstances were only made up of difficulties, if they were "absolute difficulty," we couldn't *exist,* could not mesh with them, and they would anihilate us. If, on the other hand, our circumstances were all facilities, and when I pressed my hand against a wall it gave way, I would never have any feeling or experience of resistance; that is, circumstances would be no more than an extension of myself, and I would be like God.

Man has always been aware that the element in which he must live, his circumstances, is hostile, negative. At least he has always been aware of this with the unconscious "awareness" we called "taking something for granted" when we made the distinction between *ideas* and *beliefs.*

One oblique expression of the fact that man is aware of the hostility of his ambience, without direct, formal consciousness of the fact, is symbolized by the fairy wand, and the world it creates where all our desires are automatically realized. With this symbol man communicates to himself, inadvertantly, in a reverse image, that *his* world, his real world is, at least in part, an unfavorable, anti-magic world where most of his desires are not realized. The imagery of the expulsion from Paradise is another symbol of our belief that our actual environment is far from a paradise, which would be one offering no resistance, where everything rushed to fulfill our every desire; environs that seemed in their lack of resistance, no different from ourselves—in short, an environment that belied its name. On the contrary, the world into which man is shoved, on expulsion from Paradise, is composed of obstacles. It is a foreign and negative environment with which man, for the nonce, had no idea how to deal; because it is foreign to him he doesn't know how to behave in its regard. Neither the magic world nor Paradise is an environment; still, man's real circumstances amount to an "anti-Paradise."

The fundamental "fact" we have and with which we begin is a set of circumstances, composed at one and the same time of obstacles and facilities. For example, the two segments of those circumstances nearest me are "my body" and "my soul"; for both are no more than special groupings of particular facilities and obstacles.

Thus "my body" proved two years ago that it had a particularly tough heart when the great Parisian sugeon, Dr. Grosset, approached it—"my body"—scalpel in hand, with the intention of slicing open my chest cavity and said to his assistant that he would probably kill me but that he had no choice since if he didn't operate, I would probably die anyway. But my heart survived the operation. This is an example of a facility provided my old friend, the body! But at the same time this body harbors a disastrous liver that has raked me over the coals for the last twenty years; and my nervous system is so sensitive that with the least variation in atmospheric pressure due to a change of temperature in the jungle of Upper Paraguay, I shiver here in Caballito. This is an example of an obstacle that the body represents. But it is with this body, in part favorable, in part adverse, my almost friend and nearly my enemy, that *I* have to live. It has come between me and what I have to do innumerable times; I have stumbled against it and fallen. And there are people who try to persuade me that I am this body of mine! The same thing happens with my soul. It too holds a certain repertoire of facilities and obstacles for me; but I won't speak of either grouping at this time. Out there, beyond this so called body and this so-called soul, are the so-called *animals*, *vegetables*, and *minerals*; and there are other people; all this deployed in a stage setting, an environment, a landscape.

For, as fundamental reality, the earth is simply a landscape or a series of landscapes that I inhabit.

(I have left an enormous blank in this inventory of all there is, in our circumstances, because it has to do with *something* the mode of presentation of which is so peculiar that the mere attempt to make a first descriptive pass at it would take more time than we can dream of spending now on the effort. This *something*, with its perplexing way of appearing, is God. God, if he appears, does so in the guise of a lack, as not being there, he is present as an absence. This presence is like the missing piece in a mosaic; we notice its existence because it isn't there, because we feel it as a lack. God is missing! God is the eternal absent one who must be sought. Just as the sun shines on our landscape, so God, in his absence, also sheds light on it.)

What all these names—animals, vegetables, minerals, mankind—denote, as fundamental realities, are not *things*, but what *happens to me* regarding them, as groupings of specific facilities and obstacles. However, it is only natural, in this "table of contents" to my entire philosophy, in this order or series of weak statements I have been firing off on the run, that at this point someone should ask what else, in addition to circumstances, that other ingredient is that I am. I have said that the I that I am is neither my body nor my soul, and that these are only that portion of my circumstances that is nearest me—a sort of border between my circumstances and me—which is why they are often confused with me. A border, of course, is a place where one reality ends and another begins. This is why it is a shifting, ambiguous line, a place for confusion, a terrain for military clashes that are then told in resounding border ballads. Since they are what is closest to me, body and soul are almost me, are that part of my circumstances that are most properly and characteristically mine. They are an essential property that no one can confiscate. (Parenthetically, this should be used as one of the criteria for a really serious theory of legal property.)

What am I? Fortunately, we do not need to go into this subject here; I have dealt with it repeatedly in several essays. For example, there is "Goethe from Within"; there is also a course I gave long ago, published now under the title "Meditation on Technology"; and, finally, there is the course given at the Friends of Art Circle. In that course, which I am afraid was not sufficiently understood by the intellectuals, writers, and professors in the audience, and which, even if an entirely mistaken enterprise from beginning to end, was extremely important, in that course I attempted to lay the foundation of a brand-new sociology. In that particular course—as I say—I offered a theory of the person.

For the first response to the question What am I?—as I have often said—is not that I am that *body*-thing, nor that quasi-thing, the *soul*, nor yet that super-thing resulting from an attempted union of the two. I am not a *thing* at all; I am a *person*.

One of the few ideas of Scheler's we can still accept today is his perception that the person—as he says—is only the subject of its acts as such. It isn't necessary to understand the rather hermetic meaning of these words, since, as I indicated, he merely glimpsed a truth but never fully grasped it and still less managed to conceptualize it, due to his lack of philosophical knowledge and technique. Naturally, this does not mean that Scheler, the writer, was not always a formidable thinker and one of the best minds around. But his definition of the person tells us next to nothing about it; in reality, it tells us nothing at all.

I, what is an *I*? It is a person. And what is a person? Any answer must start with the realization that it is not sufficient or adequate, in defining the person, simply to ask what the *I* is; the question must at least be modified to ask what *I* am. With more exactness, we must make further adjustment and flatly ask, who am *I?*; who, in the most specific sense of the word, is the *I* to which I repeatedly refer, not in its most abstract sense, which I use in reference to all who are an *I*, to you, to him, but rather the *I*, I myself *am* and no one else—neither you nor he.

Thus the *something* that a person is turns out to be a *someone*. That is, the *I* of each one of you consists, for the nonce, in having to listen to the next word I am going to speak. Or, if there is someone out there bent on not listening—a possibility of which I am always aware—then nevertheless his *I* is one that must avoid listening to the next word I speak. In either case it comes to the same thing: the *I* of each of you is such that it must exist in the next moment—and in a certain way: listening, or not listening, if you pursue your own musings.

That is, the consistency of the *I* is particularly strange inasmuch as it lies in being-for-the-future. *I* am that which must be, and in a certain way, one peculiar to me, in the near and the distant future. In the same way that in analyzing Cartesian *doubt* we found that many other things formed part of it, gave it meaning, now when we analyze the contents, the consistency of the *I* that each of you is, which now apparently consists solely in having to listen to my next words, we shall also find that many other things are part of it.

Indeed, it is not by chance that each of you is now an *I* that must listen to me. That *I* is out there prepared to listen or not to me, because a few hours or a few days ago it decided to be the *I* that would attend this lecture. You are not out there at blind fate's behest the way a star at this moment is at a particular point in its orbit. You are here because you came here; that is, because previously the *I* of each of you decided to be one who was coming here, who would exist, and in a certain way, in a future time that is now this lecture. Seen from our present, the *I* that decided to come here is a past one, but then it lay in the future. It was exactly the one that would spend its time in a certain way at this future time, that is to say, in the future time of this present lecture. This future time is now our present; and, as such, it is now continually turning into time past, precisely because it is "what is happening to us."

But if, in an act of memory, you analyze the *I* that was to come here, you will find it was this way: it had to come here, to spend time this way, because coming here now made sense for the one it had to be tomorrow, and so on and so forth throughout your lives. In short, at each moment, the *I* of each of you consists in a global life-project or way of being human that was adopted. *That something*, made up of a global life-project, which must *be* in its future and which today is here, in a more or less detailed way; the *figure* or *character* that has to be *that something*, is "the *person*" that each one is. Notice that to be able to say that the *I* is this, what it must be—the future person—one must first have discarded the category of substance at the appropriate time and place.

This point need detain us no longer since—I repeat—I have dealt with most of these problems elsewhere in essays. I will only add that this vital program that each of us is, is more or less distinct in each case; the individual *I* is more or less individualized and different from the others. And since *living* consists in confronting the circumstances of this program in order to be what each of us is, and since these circumstances are a repertoire of facilities and obstacles, then the same *circumstances*—if we can speak thus—will divide up into as many different circumstances as there are individuals. This is because what may be a facility for me may be an obstacle for someone else. Or, as our deep thinker Don Quixote said to dull-witted Sancho: "What looks like a barber's basin to you looks to me like a helmet, and will seem like something else to the next man."

Thus the contour of each *I* presses against its circumstances with the special profile that it has: and the circumstances will respond differently, according to these contours, warpings, and patternings of the *I* that each of us is. I said last spring that I thought it would be useful to put in circulation that lovely word *gábilo* we have, which means the section lines that are laid down—that used to be laid down—in shipyards for cutting a ship's—especially a sailing ship's—frames; in other words, the most beautiful lines in the world. Moreover, I suspect, although I can't guarantee it, that the word *gábilo* is the root of the most Spanish word of all, because its referent is the Spanish quality par excellence. I believe *garbo* [elegance of gesture] comes from *gábilo*.

We can, therefore, state all the above in common parlance by saying that the same things in our surroundings are different for each of us, even though in an abstract sense they are the same.

For example, the other day when I said it would be amusing to describe what I "was being" to each of you, or at least to the different classes of human being into which you might fall, some of you felt a blush stirring. Because one simply mustn't do that; I can't specify what I am to each person unless I also specify, reveal, at least in principle, the most intimate longings that make up each of you. You sensed, correctly, that I was threatening to violate the professional secret that each of you is. To violate is, in this case, to bring to the surface, and expose to all eyes. . . .

Let the foregoing suffice to outline—however summarily—the makeup of the two ingredients, *circumstances* and *I*, the mutuality of which makes up my life, our lives, that is, fundamental reality.

But now we must move forward with dispatch. For if the *I* is something that must exist in the near future with a contour that will mould circumstances according to its special profile, then we have accomplished in one step and without effort, a whole series of specific discoveries.

First discovery. What man is—man himself, as program and aspiration—lies in the future. What he must do is *be*, exist, tomorrow, and according to that 'I' with its peculiar profile. We have here a rather strange mode of being real, one that no traditional ontology could have understood. With traditional ontologies, a being, a reality, is, exists, precisely because what it is already exists. You will understand this easily: when a stone comes into existence, everything that makes up the stone's being or essence or consistency already exists. Thus the stone never exists merely as the aspiration to become a stone, but instead is "all stone" from the moment it begins to exist. What exists of man, on the other hand, is the need to be this or that at some future date. Each of you—I repeat—is someone who has to listen to the next word I speak; this is so because tomorrow you have to do a certain *something else*, and so on, according to the entire program of your lives, to achieve the kind of human being you have decided on. Therefore, man is first of all "someone who is not yet." He is the existence of a non-existence.

Try and see if you can describe the reality we term "aspiration" in any other way. Our aspiration has real existence now, but what exists of that aspiration is what is yet to be, what we aspire *to*, the non-existent as such. The same occurs with what is still in the future. The future only exists in the present, because *exist* and *be present* are the same thing. But what exists as the future is precisely what does not yet exist. Of that future the only thing that exists is "our expectation" and "our fear" of it. Thus man is especially futurization, is, above all, a swarm of hopes and fears.

This is the tremendous, the unavoidable paradox to which I referred earlier. Man's way of being real turns out to be just the opposite of the stone's way. The latter is everything it is, all it consists of and what exists in it. It needs nothing more. It's that way; if it weren't, there would be no *stone*.

Now then, for the Classical-Scholastic tradition in philosophy, this is the meaning of substance; *this is why substance in this tradition* is the prototype of *being*.

Descartes—as we said—against his better instincts, as I

pointed out, continued in the belief that substance is the prototype of being; and he offered a rigorous definition of substance—from a classical point of view, one he fought against in all other respects. His definition, with one exception, was more rigorous than any of those by the Greeks or the Scholastics. Descartes said: "By substance I understand only that which exists in such a way that it needs nothing more in order to exist." (The only possible precedent for such a phrase is Father Francisco Suárez's *Disputaciones Metafísicas*, when he says: "substance has no need of a subject in order to exist." And he uses the word *indigens*, the same one—*indigent*—used by Descartes. Father Suárez is one of the great thinkers in our European past, and his influence was enormous. As you know, Leibnitz declared that he had learned more philosophy from the *Disputaciones* than from any other book. I am surprised that Descartes's biographers never guessed that Descartes must have studied, must have read and learned from this book. My reason for thinking this is simple: Descartes studied at a college that had just been founded at La Fleche with the intention of making it the finest instructional institution in all France and, thus, in all Europe. That was in 1606. The date when Descartes entered La Fleche and began, therefore, to study philosophy is the publication date of the *Quixote* and of Suárez's *Disputaciones Metafísicas*, which were both to become so important. There is scant likelihood that this book, which immediately became fashionable,—because it was, and remained, the purest, most perfect expression of Scholasticism—was not studied by young men then in the avantgard, the golden youths of European thought, who, like Descartes, would usher Western man into a new world and a new conception of things.)

So that *substance* is what needs nothing else to exist. *Color* is not substance—the Greeks, the Scholastics, and Descartes would say—because in order to exist it needs a surface to cover. A substantial being is one that is not *indigens*, that needs nothing further in order to exist. Or, as I like to say: substance is sufficient being.

But here is man who is primarily "he who is not yet what he is." Who, instead, must struggle to be what he would be, fight so as to exist, and so as to exist according to his program and his aspirations. Man is now—in each successive now—exactly what he has not yet managed to become. Thus he is "what he lacks." Far from being *sufficient* being, he is *indigent* being. The only one of Aristotle's notions that is any use in defining man is his most extravagant definition of all: the concept of *privation*. Man is a network of privations. He and everything else properly human—knowledge, for example—has to be defined according to what is lacking. We define a one-armed man (a *manco*) as we do because he lacks an arm. Ontologically speaking, man is a stump.

I remember a story by Conan Doyle in which a scientist has, along with other curiosities in his laboratory, a severed hand in a beaker of alcohol. And the entire plot revolves around the pursuit of this scientist by an Indian, because the severed hand belonged to him, and he has searched the whole world over—restlessly, doggedly—trying to recover his missing hand. This makes a splendid emblem for man's essential mobility, for what keeps mankind on the *qui vive* and has caused him to advance through history! Or, as I said when I was a youth, in November of 1916 when I spoke in the lecture room of *La Prensa*: "the essence of man is," I remember I ended by saying, "discontent, divine discontent: a sort of love without a beloved, the ache we feel in a member we no longer have. . . ."

Second discovery. Since *living* amounts to having to exist in specific circumstances that are more or less opposed to me, to the *I* that *I* must be, which I lack and of which I am in need, my personal segment of indigence, then life is a labor of realization and not something that is already there, it is a task, something to be accomplished. Hence my well-known formula: Life is given us, since we find ourselves in it, without our knowing how or why; but the life that is given us is not given ready-made, and instead we have to forge it for ourselves, each one his own life. Life is something we *must do*, and it gives us a lot *to do!*

In an essay of mine, "History as System," I show that to my way of thinking life is not a fact, not a *factum*, but a *faciendum*, something that has to be accomplished; it is not a substantive but a gerund. And yesterday I was deeply moved, on rereading *Amadís de Gaula*—in a nice Argentine edition, although the print is too small—to see that Amadís, "the Fair Youth of the Sea," or, as he is also called, with deep and acute poetry, "Amadís without Time," says about himself, speaking about what he has done, his life: that it is his *hacienda*. This *hacienda* is the *faciendum*, the gerund, what has to be done. . . .

Therefore, since these circumstances are foreign, heterogeneous, they are always in opposition to the realization of the *I* that is ever urging its profile of aspirations upon them. Now then, in my effort *to be*, in wanting *to be*, what I seek is *to be happy*. *Happiness*, that strange and inadequately explained basic need that man has, would then lie in our managing to realize the program of our life, the *I* that we are. However, since our circumstances always oppose us, the *I* we are is never sufficiently accomplished; man, whose life consists in needing to be happy is always, to a degree, *unhappy*.

This is why life is suffering, continual suffering. Precisely because it is, already, previously, the desire to be, enthusiasm and hope.

A being not consisting in aspirations could not be unhappy. Man is a utopian being who only tries to be "the impossible." By this I mean to be, given his circumstances—whether they be called *world* or *nature*—the impossible; and when he tries to realize this *in* his circumstances he bumps into *that*. The permanent bruise he gets from that bump is "unhappiness."

Hence the feeling of enchantment and envy we sometimes feel when we contemplate the peacefulness of animals living in their natural habitat! We envy them not because they are happy—animals aren't happy—we envy them because they are not unhappy; they "fit" their ambiance. Animals are *adapted*, while man is essentially *unadapted*. Man is everywhere a foreigner.

Third discovery. This definition of life—in part sad and deficient—and yet true, is not the whole truth. Because, obviously, if life were only this, we would leave it as soon as we got here. Never forget it is always possible for man to exit from life. That exit has a horrible name that I won't mention, but it is one of the constitutional possibilities of human life. Thus if man does not abandon his life, he accepts the defects, mischance, unhappiness, the absolute risk that it is. And if he accepts it——Well then! He transforms the defects and mischance into an enthusiastic undertaking, into adventure and enterprise.

So that in my doctrine of life we discover the indissoluble conjunction—in no way contradictory, just the reverse— the mutual need of synthesis that the two great truths about human life have. I refer to the Christian truth, according to which "life" is a vale of tears; and the Pagan truth, which makes a *stádion* for sports of that vale of tears.

Life as anguish, Mr. Heidegger? Agreed! But, it is also this: an enterprise.

To repeat my argument: for there to be anguish, I must be alive. If I give up life, anguish ceases and life as well. But if I stay with life this means I accept its painful, its anguished task. And this willing acceptance of painful effort is the very definition of athletic striving.

5

A way of thinking that decided the destiny of the West. The question: What is reality? Things, change, movement. Heraclitus and Parmenides. Concept and identity. The ukase of Parmedides. Being, intellectualized. The great rationalists. The collision of two bodies. Return to Greece. Aristotle. The idea of nature. Logical knowledge. A reform of the intellect's mission. The *ponendo tollens* mode. The fruitfulness and insufficiency of Eleaticism. Man has no nature. Being as "having been thus and so." Historical Reason appears.

IN THE PRECEDING LECTURES I made a special effort to have things not only clear but also easy to understand. This does not mean that today I shall do any less; but since I must condense a great amount of thought into a few minutes, while I may manage to be clear I doubt it will be possible to make things easy. We have to deal with difficult questions concerning the techniques of thought that are more than weighty; but their difficulty lies not in their being highly technical, just the opposite. We have no alternative but to assume the rigor and difficulty of their technicality, because only with the precise apparatus of that technicality will we be able to solve the problems that today engulf humanity.

I therefore ask permission to address myself especially to

the professors, students, and amateurs of philosophy. Let
me be, just this once, the gray old professor of philosophy!
Let me deliver a lecture entirely devoid of brilliance! Quite
soon those who expect other things of my lectures will, I
hope, find them when, in a few days, I take up again the
exposition of my sociological thought under my accustomed
title, "Lectures of Man and People."We shall speak there of
other subjects that are equally rigorous and difficult, but
more concrete, lively, and scintillating. We shall speak there
of the disguises of social modes, the relations between the
individual and the collective, of what I call "collective norms,"
of what people say—that is, ordinary speech and public
opinion—of law and state, nation and internation, and even
ultra-nation; this last being the phenomenon of the
future.Because a new kind of collectivity is being created
today that is not the "internation" and not the "internation-
ality," neither of which exists or can exist as a collectivity—
and anyone who says otherwise is not aware of what he is
saying—but instead a series of "ultra-nations."
   Speaking of "ultra": the ultra-weightiness of the philosophical reform that what I have been saying implies cannot
be clearly grasped unless we go back to the beginning of
philosophy, back twenty-seven hundred years ago in Greece.
. . . In this way we shall find that the entire history of the
West constitutes a single unit, which has been what it has
been—that is, has had the history it has had—because twenty-
seven hundred years ago the Greeks adopted a particular
mode of thought. As we shall see, they might have adopted
a different one, and then the history of mankind would have
been very different; but the former way triumphed, and
when it did, when the mode of thinking I refer to triumphed,
the one to be examined in this lecture, the destiny of twenty-
seven hundred years of human history was inexorably and
prophetically fixed. If now we were to adopt a radically,
formally "other" mode of thinking, just imagine the poten-

tial value of the reform, and the vast new horizons open to human destiny, toward which the eager finger of hope would then point.

The history of philosophy began with what Plato termed a "giantomachy," in the tremendous struggle between two titans of thought: Heraclitus of Ephesus and Parmenides of Elea. Everything that precedes these two, from Thales of Miletus on down, is still not *philosophy*, and the Greeks themselves called it *physiology*. Physiology is merely the preparation for and the preamble to philosophy; the latter properly begins with the struggle between Heraclitus and Parmenides, the two great Saurian intellectuals.

The question confronting man, the human mind, is, what is there? The task is to discover what way we have of describing what is there in rigorous—philosophical—concepts. But what is there? What do we have round about us? Before me I see a *stone*, but I also see *movement* in space when this stone is flung from a sling. I see Socrates at a banquet; but I also see that, halfway through dinner, Socrates—Athens' heaviest drinker—has a bright red face, bright red from the alcohol; but then I see by first light that while all the other feasters lie under their tables, only Socrates remains fresh and upright, albeit rather pale. (Plato tells all this in the *Symposium*.)

So, there is *Socrates*; but there is also Socrates *changing color*—the change in the color of his complexion: first bright red, now pale gray—so that there is *qualitative change*. There is the *stone*; but the stone was also formerly in one place and is now in another, so that there is, then, *movement*, or *change of place*; and since space is homogeneous, and these places can be *measured* and therefore *counted*, there is also *quantitative change*.

What *is*, the *real*—our goal—we termed "what there is." Very well, what is there? What do we find round about us? *Things* and *change*, *change* and *things*; all equally real. But are these two realities of equal value? For, when we try to define the primary and generic character of these two realities, we find they possess opposing features: a thing is always there, immediately apparent to the eye: equal to itself, self-identical; whereas change, movement, is not identical and is always different from itself. Thus we have two primary types of reality with opposing characteristics.

In truth, something I look at is not always the same, especially if I observe it for long enough and with sufficient attention. Socrates may have the same appearance throughout the day, except for the change of color in his face when he drinks and when he abstains—now bright red, now a pale gray. But if I wait awhile, a few years, I shall see how Socrates, yesterday with a young body, today, mature, and tomorrow old, becomes decrepit, and later a corpse; then the corpse will decompose, disintegrate, and if we wait even longer we will see his bones become dust and be scattered by the air, so that of the identity and self-sameness of Socrates nothing will remain. . . .

Therefore, these two kinds of reality, *things* and *change*, have each a different status, and when we contemplate them, as they come under observation and are closely observed, we notice that peaceful, stable being becomes movement and flux; that its permanence is not confirmed, but rather the stable and identical is found to consist of mutableness and change; that self-identical being must be broken down into a truer reality: movement and flux. Everything is in flux. We cannot step twice into the same river. In truth, the *real* is like a torrent that ceaselessly passes, passes, and is not permanent at all; stability, the identical, the permanent, is only a transitory optical illusion.

This was the splendid intuition granted Heraclitus of Ephesus at the beginning of philosophy and the history of Western thought!

However, if movement and change are easy to see—you

have but to open your eyes or recall, when you see what is there now, how it was before, and to notice *quantum mutatus ab illo*—if movement and change are easy to see, they are hard to conceptualize.

If I say that something is *movement*, I am saying it is *A* but that it is also *B*, for it has changed. And since to be *B* is to be "not being *A*" or "not *A*," to say something is *movement* or *change* is to say it is "*A*" and "not *A*." This is why I said that movement is "non-identical," which is to say, "contradictory."

If I say "it is this" when I think of something as movement, I contradict myself, since I have to say it is both "*A*" and "not-*A*." What I say is self-contradictory; my thought has to unthink itself, analyze itself. If, in order to think of something as "*A*," once I have already thought of it as "not-*A*," I must cancel my previous thought, erase it, unthink it, make believe it was never thought, I am faced with a very difficult task. Of course, when I think of something as movement I am not supposed to unthink what I previously thought, but instead—when I deem something *change*—I must think both thoughts at once: *A* and not-*A;* in spite of their being incompatible I must do my best to keep them in mind together! This is why I said it was very easy to observe *change* but extremely difficult to conceptualize it—so difficult that it brought movement, variation, dizziness to the Greeks. And Zeno's arguments against movement, negating movement and variation and plurality, created such a profound effect that the Greek mind remained ensnared by them and extremely confused. This is the truth.

Heraclitus glimpsed the necessity of reducing quiet stable being to mutable, changing being; the necessity of defining being as not-being at the same time, in short as being that ceases to be: as becoming. But Heraclitus' attempt, undertaken with insufficient intellectual technique, in that first, unsteady hour of Western thought—since it was both marvelous and seminal—was doomed to fail.

Then the other giant, Parmendes, decided to undertake the opposite course: reduce all change and movement to stable being, to identity, denying straight out, heroically and by fiat, all change, mutability, movement, and flux; so he called change a mere illusion of the senses.

In the last lecture I gave in Madrid, in 1935, I discussed this very matter; and by reading and improvising I am going to use the typescript, recorded by a student and corrected by me, in developing today's subject.

I said then that if instead of taking "the observable," what the senses convey to us, we turn our backs on "what is there," close ourselves up in our thought or reason, and pay attention only to its imperatives—that is, if we decide or believe beforehand that true reality must be as our thought or reason dictates—we will discover the following situation: thought, intellect is the only reality in the universe that actually consists in identity. All else changes, varies, flows, more or less, sooner or later; on the other hand, when I think *whiteness*, I only think *whiteness*, and the *whiteness* thought, qua thought—that is, as the concept of whiteness—is invariable; my thought, *whiteness*, rejects, repels everything that is not itself; it will not tolerate being a little red, a little blue, a little black. All concepts, then, are *identity*. I could say that every concept is made of the stuff of *identity*. Of course, if when I say, or when I think, *whiteness*, I am unable to think anything but purest white, this does not mean that the real thing about which I have said this— snow, for example, a swan's feather, ermine—must needs be only white, and may not include, in addition to whiteness, a little black, some blue, and some red. In fact it is true that there is no real thing that is only white; it is an approximate white, a white mixed with other things, an almost white, or as the expression hereabouts goes, it is well-nigh white.

The white thing we see before us is not only white, it is *white* and *not-white*, that is, blue, red, black; whiteness is only one of its visible attributes. Since, in fact, this *whiteness* element is in it, our intellect discovers it there, thinks it; or, more graphically put, since I persist in my aim to be clear: the intellect seizes the element *whiteness* of the *white* and *not-white* thing, indisolubly mixed together there with blue and red, and so forth; it seizes, which is to say notices, which is to say grasps, that and only *that*. When the intellect picks something out, it fixes it, fixes it as if touching it with a magic wand, isolates, purifies, and hardens it, so that it is only *whiteness*, ever equal to itself, always identical.

This operation of fixing on an element of inexhaustible reality and fixing it or making it self-identical, of "identifying" it, is usually called "abstraction." And to "abstract," to seize something that is actually mixed together with many other things and to render it virtual or ideally isolated and alone, is the primary and basic activity of the intellect. This intellect, then, is an apparatus—I stress this. It is a mechanism for identification, for identifying reality; what, by itself, is this or that, never identical, pure variation, being what it is not, not being what it is—in a word, complete confusion. The intellect separates it into identical elements; the intellect does a marvelous, artful job of carving—the metaphor is Plato's—like the chef at a restaurant, the intellect cuts the chicken of reality into pieces, and these pieces that were not only together but were constantly changing size, shape, and consistency are separated and put in the refrigerator—that's what the intellect is—and there frozen so they are self-identical, self-consistent, fixed and unchanging. This is the way the intellect works on reality. And inevitably so. The intellect works this way automatically, and no other way; this is how it is; its law and its unswerving conduct.

Thus the earliest Greek thought had to contend with two worlds: that of visible things, which was all movement, variation, and mutability, and that of quasi-things, which was all concepts, that is, identical, invariable, and fixed. This gave rise to the event that was to decide the future for three thousand years: from the seventh century B.C. to the present.

Heraclitus and Parmenides were the first to realize that in addition to the world of things offered by the senses there is a peculiar *inwardness* that man carries around with him: the world of concepts. But, confronted by this duality, they reacted in opposite ways and collided with each other: hence, what we have called a "giantomachy."

When he discovered this world of concepts, Parmenides—the first man to notice the existence of "thought"—felt an almost religious awe, very like the one a revelation causes. Because, alongside the visible world of the senses (all unending variation, where nothing is quiet and clearly what "it is," but is instead confusion, a world where the mind—and, hence, man—can neither rest nor touch bottom), he found himself on the threshold of a divine-seeming world, "a world of concepts," where what is, is only what it is, exactly, without adulteration, and forever: a world that was substantively intelligible, transparent. Of course it was! Since concepts themselves are the product of the intellect, or pure reason.

Of all these concepts, the principal one was that of *being*, and the concept *being*—like any other—excludes what is not itself, rejects non-being, the way white did what was non-white; with the result that Parmenides, on the basis of the above line of reasoning, concluded something seemingly banal, which was the following: only *being* is, and *non-being* is not. Why? Because *non-being* cannot be thought of as *being;* that would be contradictory. His conclusion was no less than the following: only what is governed by the rules of thought is *real.* In Parmenides' reaction this was what was decisive for human history; but opposing it is the counter-decision we will be making.

What this means is no less than the following: we can only legitimately call *real* what is ruled by the laws of thought;

the key to reality lies in the inner workings of the intellect; the former, not the data of the senses, is the way, the direction, the method. For the first time in the history of philosophy the term *method* is used, and it will ever after be associated with philosophy. Thought, in the sense of intellect, is the method or way that helps us discover authentic reality. And since the *intellect*, the *concept*, consists in identity, *being*, the *real will likewise consist in identity*. This is the ukase, the decree that decided twenty-seven hundred years of history.

So Parmenides discovered that the concept, thinking, was ruled and, what is more, made up of the principle of identity; and so it was, at least to some degree. Yet the reservation implied by my last words heralds a matter so portentous I will hold it in reserve so as not to give you vertigo. It is established, then, that pure identity constitutes thought.

But not content with this, Parmenides supposed—because this was unsupported by evidence—that being, the real, was *also* made up of identity. The rationale for this transposition of the law of the intellect to the law of reality was that otherwise the real would—as we say—be "unthinkable," unintelligible. Knowledge is only possible if there is an affinity between the object to be known and the activity—reason—that consists in knowing, in short, if the *real* is also rational. To anticipate a little at this point, let me enter two remarks: first, no magic or divine power ever guaranteed that the real was *thinkable*, that we could in fact know it; second, it is equally arbitrary to suppose that for something to be intelligible it must be more or less like the intellect. Furthermore, one ought *a limine* and as a matter of course to suspect that the special problem of knowledge lies in the fundamental difference between what is to be known and the instrument of knowing. Otherwise, *knowledge* would not be particularly interesting; what *is* interesting is that even though the *real* is foreign to the intellect or pure reason, man can still fathom it, that even though *reality* is opaque, man is at all able to illuminate, to make it transparent, radiant.

In this manner Parmenides intellectualized being, and this decision—I repeat—sealed the fate of three thousand years of human history. The doctrine of being as such, ontology, has continued until now to be a doctrine of being-as-identity. Eleatic ontology (Parmenides was from Elea).

Even recently, Nicolai Hartmann, my fellow student, close friend, and for a long time now one of the two or three most outstanding philosphers in Germany—he holds the important Chair in Berlin—insisted, more than he ever had in previous books, that knowledge is impossible if the structure of reality is not at least similar to the structure of the intellect. I am truly sorry to have to disagree with my old friend, this friend of my youth with whom I spent long hours discussing Parmendes during the snowbound winters at Marburg.

Now, I have indicated that the reason for this transfer of the law of the intellect, of identity, to being is in no way justified, is without warrant; in other words, the basic supposition here, on which all else depends, is itself . . . irrational. It is merely a belief *(creencia)* that held the Greeks of the seventh century in thrall, and mankind, under the brilliant, tyrannical influence of Ancient Greece, has never managed to shake it off.

But this belief is in error. Of course it is true that the *consistency* of the concept is *identity*. (To suggest that not even thought is identity would be to open that abyss I wanted to shield you from before.) Let us agree that concepts are self-identical and therefore strictly rational, logical. By *rational* or *logical* I understand what has always been understood, that is, the intellect in its internal characteristic function, what it is in itself, for itself, and on its own, in short, pure intellect or pure reason. Logic, the science of the concept, is therefore *strictly rational*. But even numbers, *in their essence*, contain irrationalities, that is, contradictions. In fact, irrationality as such was discovered in mathematics, and the term *irrational number* was invented; as far as the Greeks were concerned it was "a scandal of nature." The *being* of spatial shapes—that is, geometry—contains even more irrationalities, even more illogicalities, inasmuch as geometry is much less logical, since space itself is essentially irrational, because continuous: a *Labyrinthum difficultatum continui*, according to Leibnitz (a "labyrinth of the difficulties of continuousness"). What Leibnitz with his eighteenth-century, rococo elegance called "the labyrinth" is what, in the tattered style of our day, or at least mine, I referred to as "complete confusion."

The continuous can be divided into parts. I can divide a continuum, such as the space taken up by this table, into parts; but those parts into which it can be divided are not, strictly speaking, parts; because in turn those parts make a continuum I can always divide again; they are not the single, individual elements that authentic parts would be. So the continuum at the same time is and is not made of parts, infinitely divisible and therefore never entirely divided; in other words, divisible and indivisible. It is therefore a superlative example of self-contradictory *being*, that is, at once A and not-A.

However logical or rational, mathematics is still in large measure illogical and irrational. In physics the degree of irrationality increases considerably; in every direction we discover irrational elements. Here is an extreme example: pure reason feels it has rendered the opaque—the problematic—transparent, intelligible and rational when it treats the opaque as a compound and analyzes it, breaking it down into simple elements. This process of reducing the complex to simplicity is what Descartes, Spinoza, Leibnitz, and Kant—the great rationalists of pure reason—called "understanding," or reason.

The extreme example, as I said, in physics is the following: the ideal, rational interpretation of sensible phenomena, which was the prototype of the sciences of reality for three hundred years, was a mechanical interpretation; *light, heat, sound,* and so forth, the *apparent world,* were explained by the collision of atoms. A phenomenon was *rationalized,* explained, or understood when it had been reduced to the simplest possible fact of two minute bodies—two atoms—in collision.

But the truth is that what occurs when two bodies collide, the transmission of movement from one to the other, is entirely mysterious and unintelligible. This is not self-evident, but rather such a commonplace event that it has precipitated in us a genuine expectation; which is why when we build on this "fact," our minds find repose. Nevertheless, this event, this "fact," what happens when two bodies collide, in spite of its frequency and usualness, is itself opaque, irrational. Reason cannot explain why one billiard stops when it strikes another, or why the second billiard darts away; this habitual event might just as well happen in the opposite way: when the first billiard strikes, the second one remains still and the first one bounces back, as happens, for example, when it is struck by the cue with what is called—I'm not certain you use the same expression—"backspin." Or, there is also another possibility that is just as legitimate as the other two: we might be accustomed to seeing the two billiards in collision remaining quietly together, "kissing" in a loving cinematic embrace. The reason why neither of the last two possibilities occurs, while the first one does, remains today not only unexplained but inexplicable. It is a simple "fact" that our senses convey or tell us about. Every occurrence is something that is told to us; every fact or occurrence is narrated. When pure reason or intelligence reduces all phenomena to that of a collision in order to understand them, it reduces them to something, therefore, that is unintelligible and irrational, to a basic event, a narrative.

But let us return to Greece. Parmenides, with that blind radicalness that usually characterizes innovators, starting with the principle that what is rational and thinkable is real, and that only what excludes change and is identical is thinkable, goes on to deny the reality of change, of movement, plurality, and so forth. Plato, who had a profoundly Eleatic soul, makes some concessions: true being, the *ontos on*, is still *identical*, but he allows that *being* may be plural, that being is not a single indivisible being, as Parmenides, with his absolute view of identity, believed, but rather consists in infinite identities: there is pure whiteness, pure justice; there is pure equality, pure good, pure beauty, which are always what they are. These identities, in which authentic reality is to be found, are the Platonic "Ideas."

Parmenides' extremism, then, leads him to deny movement, to deny the plurality of the things surrounding us; but it is not enough to deny; what is denied must also be explained. It was necessary, then, to clarify the nature of the world of "non-being" that surrounds us; if it is illusion, this illusion will have to be explained, something that neither Parmenides nor his disciples could do.

Aristotle, tired of absolute positions, and with his cold observer's eye, was not disposed to give up the reality of the things around us: the reality of this horse, this man. For the Greeks, ever since Parmenides—I repeat—whatever changed, ceased to be; what was later different from what it once was, was not worthy of the name "being." Yet the horse and the man constantly changed qualities and place; this meant they were not being. Would it not be possible to discover something unchanging in these realities, something of that stillness, that enormous stillness that "being" was for the Greeks? Was there no way to find in the unquiet and the mutable, "something" unchanging, in repose, that "*was?*"

Let us observe the variations of things to see if they are

limitless. Is not change, are not the differences, in the horse, more or less unlike those in man? In point of fact, the changes in each species of reality—man, animal, vegetable, mineral, stone, and star—constitute different specific repertoires of variations. Each thing, then, is variation; but its variety is invariable: A star moves, but its movement is uniform.

Well then! It could well be that beneath things' change-able appearances, a latent principle exists that is the law of their variations and the latter's cause; a being, then, that is stable and quiet, underlying their unstable and unquiet appearances.

This invariable law of a thing's variations, the unstable being's stable being, the identical being that seems to lie behind the contradiction, is *physis*, the physical substance or nature of a thing. This concept of *nature* that Aristotle cre-ated refers, therefore, to everything and is simply the prin-ciple of identity he feels is the law and cause of each thing's variations, behind the untameable flux of its appearances.

If we pursue this point further, we see that Stoicism and Epicureanism, instead of speaking of the nature of each thing, speak of the nature of all things together, collectively, and then we have the idea of "nature," or natural universe, the *natura rerum*.

But is this idea of nature being applied to each thing in particular or to the whole? Remember that *nature* means "the invariable law" of variable things, or "the identical" in the contradictory, since it was no more and no less than a modification or softening of Eleaticism at Aristotle's hands. It was an idea constructed on the basis of the belief that the real has to have something identical about it, has to be, in some sense, equal to itself—the way concepts are—in short, that the *ordo et connexio idearum idem est ac ordo et connexio rerum*, that "the order and connection of things is the same as the order and connection of our ideas," as Spinoza would say in the eighteenth century. With this assertion, as it happens, identity is raised to the third power; because this establishes (1) the identity of the concept, which is evident; (2) the identity of the concept and the real; and (3) the consequent identity of reality. The first—I repeat—is evident, the other two are mere supposition.

The idea of nature evolves, is refined, and with Robert Boyle, in the eighteenth century, in England, it looses its status as mysterious latent cause of visible variations and is left with its reputation as a pure law of the variations; Aristotle's *natura* is stylized as a simple law of nature. And if we advance a century and a half more we find old, mysterious, tremendous nature become for Positivism—that is, for Comte and John Stuart Mill—little more than the invariability itself of the laws of nature. This ghost is all that remains of that almost religious idea of nature that was Aristotle's. . . . But for that very reason this ghost shows all the more clearly its original content, which was identity pure and simple.

For Positivism, this invariableness of the phenomena, of movements and change, was nothing—*is* nothing, since it is still the ruling doctrine in the laboratory—but a proposition, albeit one on which nothing less than the whole of our knowledge depends; but Positivism realizes it can't be proved, that it is irrational. (Strictly speaking, whenever we say something is a proposition, we mean little more than a belief we inhabit, without knowing how or why.)

But if, for contemporary science, nature means only the invariability of observable phenomena, then nature is no more than a man-made hypothesis invented at a certain date and must run its course like everything human and pass away. . . . This is why philosophy, when it must describe fundamental reality, cannot base itself on, or take seriously the concepts of, the natural sciences; because, as we said, they are hypotheses concerning reality, not authentic reality itself.

Even though it sounds paradoxical, and I am sorry time doesn't allow me to explain it: physics is not knowledge of reality itself, but only a useful working hypothesis. The truth of physics is not in its theory; it lies in its resulting practical applications. As I said in the second lecture, scientific theory has a cutting edge, not in itself but in its practice, its application.

And I went on to say in the lecture I referred to that I termed all thought from Parmenides to the present "naturalism"; because all thought has maintained, believed—Hegel is no exception that the mission of the intellect is to search in reality for what is identical. But this means an exercise of knowing that begins with two assumptions: first, that reality has the same consistency as the intellect, or, as we have often said, that its *being* is being identical; second, something we have not said before, that in order to know, intelligence must function according to its internal, domestic, and private law, which is the principle of identity, in short, logic, reason self-absorbed, pure reason. *To know*, then, the ideal of knowing, would be to let the intelligence function according to its own law, that is, in exclusively logical fashion. Together these two things mean that *knowing* is adapting reality to the intellect, and not just the reverse—which is what I shall now formally maintain: that *knowing* is, by every means at our command, and reason is the foremost of these, to adapt ourselves and especially to adapt our use of reason to reality. Or, to put this difficult, very difficult, idea another way: if by thought we understand not only the intelligence but the whole business of knowing, of knowing by different means, whatever they may be, we must needs follow with all possible rigor the laws of logic, of the intelligence. But that once this is done, we will not have done anything important or positive as far as knowing is concerned; this is merely the *conditio sine qua non*. The true task begins when thinking attempts to adapt logic, which is *intelligence*, to the illogical thing that *reality* is; in other words, that thought, without its intelligence ceasing to be logical,

to be pure reason, be obliged to be *itself*—thought, not intelligence—illogical. Yet this heralds no more and no less than
the most radical reform imaginable to date in the theory of
knowledge, because it implies not the need to transform this
or that cog or method of intelligence, but the need to entirely
rectify the very relationship between all intelligence and
reality.

Until now, knowing meant believing that what intelligence thinks about things is their truth, or, and it comes to
the same thing, that the mission of our ideas, of the intelligence, is to reproduce in one way or another, to contain the
being or *consistency* of things, either the total being, as rationalism believed, or, at least, the partial being, as Kant and
Positivism held. But the part of my theory of knowledge that
effects a substantial modification of this is the very mission
of the intelligence, its role in the task of knowing. According to my theory, we never think reality itself; because what
we think is logical, and reality is illogical. What we think is
merely the instrument by which we are able to see, to intuit,
to make reality patent. The intelligence provides us with a
topographical map that enables us to reach a certain landscape without losing ourselves therein; but the reality of the
landscape is not there on the map, which is an unreal schema,
but rather what we see of it with our eyes. When it is a
question of incorporeal realities, then our *seeing* is likewise
incorporeal, extra-sensory; it would be what *in genere* is called
"intuition."

Knowing, then, is a round-trip voyage: first we must form
ideas—notice this—about things, which is what has been
done until now; but then, to truly know, it is necessary to
subtract all that has been thought, in the realization that
reality is always more or less different from what was thought.
One must *know*, therefore, by making substantive use of
what logicians used to call the *modus ponendo tollens*, the "mode
of denying by affirming," the enunciatory mode in which,

at one and the same time, we take back what we assert. In order to overcome the radical foreignness of *being*, of the *real*, thinking must subtract itself, remove, or as one might say, remove from reality, what it has put there, which is always a falsification of reality inasmuch as it is nothing if not exaggeration. Henceforth the *modus ponendo tollens* will be the key signature of all knowledge theory, and since we are in Buenos Aires, and as an homage to this city, I wouldn't at all mind naming my theory of knowledge as follows: the gnoseological theory of "almost up to here"—since this expression is a perfect model of what I have called, and what logic terms, the *modus ponendo tollens*, of taking away by positing, of positing by taking away.

We must therefore abandon Parmenides, with his inveterate and tenacious Eleaticism, and once again take our departure from Heraclitus, reworking his failed gesture with finer instruments. The real is the non-identical, it is pure event, mobility, flux. This is why we need, why we have evolved a non-Eleatic ontology, just as Einstein created a non-Euclidean and a non-Archimedean physics.

To suppose, along with the entire Eleatic tradition of philosophy, that the real is intelligible in its very structure is a vicious circle and ignores, moreover, the inherent drama of knowledge. Intelligence is an instrument for knowing, and there is no likelihood—above all, there is no guarantee—that the reality to be known bears any resemblance to the instrument used in knowing it. Until now, thinking in this way has been like looking at one microscope through another one just like it, instead of looking at the very "opposite" of a microscope, which is a cell.

The three expressions—Eleaticism, identicalism, and rationalism—all mean the same thing, where one begins by projecting the law of the intellect onto being, and then the intellect draws back from the real just what it had projected onto it. This always reminds me of an amusing fin-de-siècle story by the French humorist Courteline, the story of the good French bourgeois who, like so very many good French bourgeois, was both vain and a fisherman. This good bourgeois fisherman had a trained shad and on holiday would go to the shore and throw it overboard. When some passer-by came near the good man, he would lean down the bank and, with his hand to his mouth, call out: "Bite, Theodore!" And the good, trained shad would find the hook, allow himself to get caught on it, and come forth flapping its tail in the breeze, astonishing the passer-by and satisfying the vanity of the good bourgeois fisherman. Now then, in this allegory the *reality* is the flowing current—Heraclitus was the first to compare reality with a river, in which it is impossible to step twice—the shad is that *intellectual identity* we extract from our heads and toss into that reality, and *knowledge* is the elegant operation of fishing the trained shad from the place wherein he was thrown.

Nonetheless, Eleaticism has thus far been both necessary and fruitful. Necessary, because man in centuries past did not possess, especially in early Greece and medieval times, adequate methods of thought that would permit him to behave any differently vis-à-vis reality. For this reason, it was necessary, useful, but also fruitful. Because in fact when we make a first, rough approach to reality—especially physical reality, or sensory reality, the phenomena usually called "natural"—it does respond as if it were governed by identity; but as soon as physics begins to use more precise instruments it falters and discovers irrationality, the nonidentity of nature. This is the real reason for what is called "the indeterminacy of the atom," which today has caused such deception in modern quantum theory, and a veritable malaise in physics, as well as "the crisis of the principles of physics."

But if naturalism has begun to fail in physics, it has always failed where man was concerned. Naturalism or Eleaticism, when it addresses anything, has no choice—since this is the method that constitutes it—but to search for a nature, an identity in its object; this is why, in setting out to study man, it tried to discover his nature. But, we don't know why, man has never taken the hook the way the fisherman's shad did. And for three consecutive centuries, using all possible forms and methods, it has utterly failed to unearth man's nature. A few years ago, when a profound shift began to affect Western man, when we first began not to know what was happening to *us*—not to Sirus, not to the galaxies, about which science knows so much—we asked science what had happened to man. But science kept silent, because it had no answer at all.

This is one explanation for the uncertainty today—I don't think it can be anything else—of our faith, our belief in reason. But this simply means that perhaps man has no nature, that is, no identity. And all we have said amounts to the discovery and the assertion of this—this radical real ity, that life, we said, instead of being, is actually a being *and* unbeing, an occurring, a transit, a continual flux. Today man is as he is precisely because yesterday he was something else; the mature man is *mature* because he was *young*, and he continues to be young in the mode of once *having been young*. If you could excise the youth that he was from the mature man, and which he continues to be in the mode of having-been-so, a mature man would become an adolescent. What is more, the return to infancy in old age happens because the old man no longer remembers, that is, no longer retains what he was, and so must begin over, become a child again, start a new life.

Actually, this has always been man's condition: he has been first one thing and then another; he pursued one ideal, used it up, and because he had exhausted it and because of the experience that accrued, he pursued another. Man has undertaken the most diverse forms of being; because, to the despair of the intellectualists, man is *happenstance*. He has one thing after another happen to him: he happens to be a stoic, a Christian, a rationalist, a positivist, to be what he is about to be now. . . . Man is the female of the Paleolithic from which Madame Pompadour eventually emerged; he is the Brazilian Indian who can only count up to five; and he is Henri Poincaré and Newton, Genghis Khan and Saint Francis, Pericles and Charlie Chaplin.

Man undergoes, traverses, all these forms of being; a pilgrim of being, he goes along, being and un-being them, that is, living them. Man has no nature; what he has is history; because *history* is the mode of being of the entity that is constitutionally, fundamentally, *mobility* and *change*. And this is why pure, Eleatic, naturalistic reason will never manage to understand man. This is why, until now, man has remained an unknown. Because history is the mode of being of an entity that is fundamentally variable and without identity. Man cannot be *identi-fied*. He a metaphysical Arsène Lupin.

Man is an "unknown," and he will not be discovered in the laboratories. The hour of the historical sciences is at hand. Pure reason (which, as we noticed, ended its attempt to deduce everything according to pure logic by basing itself on the narrative of an event: the collision of atoms) must be replaced by narrative reason. *Today* man is as he is because *yesterday* he was something else. Therefore, to understand what he is today we have only to relate what he was *yesterday*. That is enough, and here we have, come to light, just what we are doing here. This narrative reason is "historical reason."

Time has run out. We reach a point where historical reason looms before us, but without reaching it. Not much we can do about that! Recall the phrase of Seneca's that Schopenhauer so admired that he used it as the epigraph of one of his books: "If anyone, after running all day, arrives at nightfall, it is more than enough. . . ."

Historical Reason
(Lisbon, 1944)

1

Reservations about the eulogy of an intellectual.
Does the intellectual possess his intelligence? Is
intelligence a matter of chance? Intelligence cannot be professionalized. The changed social status of the intellectual. Progress and intelligence.
My premonition and its fulfillment. The extra
piece. The peculiar ancient figure of the intellectual. The prophet in Israel. Two mental sets.
The novelty of intellectual method.

YOU HAVE HEARD how the director has greeted my possession of this Chair, and the kindness and deference of his
words will be obvious to all. Not so obvious is what lies
behind them—that is, the interest on Dr. Oliveira Guima-
rães' part that made this course possible, an interest that led
him to think it up with Professor Victoriano Nemesio as
well as offer the salutory words of a few moments ago. So
if the lectures proceed with good fortune and amount to
something substantive in the intellectual life of this Faculty
of Humanities—instead of being a futile ornament and a
routine exercise if these lectures, as I say, produce some
appreciable and productive impact on the Portuguese mind,
which for the moment is not something either the speaker
or his listeners can be certain of, all the credit will go to the
director of this Faculty. Pointing this out, in addition to
being de rigueur, gives me a chance to open a parenthesis of
cordiality that will permit me to respond directly to his kind

words. In part they referred to the general outline of my thought or philosophical doctrine. I need not say I approve and subscribe to all he said in this regard. But the rest of his words consisted of homage and praise of my intellectual stature. And this is something that, without it being his intention, obliges me to begin our acquaintance by taking up a difficult problem, inasmuch as his words of eulogy place me squarely on the horns of the following recalcitrant dilemma: although I wish to thank him for them I can't accept them. The first point is self-evident—and is not in question—because there are things that are completed in their desiring, and so it is with thanks. But the second is less obvious: why should I object when generosity and benevolence send praise my way? Clearly, I am not mounting the trapeze of false modesty; not at all. There are more exemplary reasons and ones of higher caliber for my scruples and reservations.

Here is the first one. To eulogize is undoubtedly a beautiful and fruitful activity—but for this very reason its use must be qualified; at least, the object of the eulogy must be a perfect match for it. We eulogize and praise an individual for having some outstanding quality. So the quality must be outstanding, and the individual who possesses it too. It is customary to praise an intellectual for his intelligence. But I ask myself the following: if we use words with care, can we say the intellectual possesses his intelligence the way he does the coins in his pocket? Is intelligence, taken as a modus operandi, appropriately spoken of as something we possess; and does it justify the notion of possession, the mere hybrid imperialism that ownership is? It is certainly correct to say that a truly beautiful young woman *possesses* her beauty, because it shines and radiates from her endlessly, without interruption or eclipse, day after day, hour after hour, perhaps with a slight oscillation of intensity and a gentle undulation in its perfection. The beautiful woman can be certain of the magic dynamism of her beauty. It is always at her command, she is mistress of it with a complete, easy possessiveness, because the quality, the beauty functions like a marvellous and perpetual radioactivity, freed of any limitation.

Now then, this is by no means the case with the intelligence of even the most intelligent of intellectuals. At best, he is able, in a retrospective review of his past, to confirm that on this, that, or the other occasion, he behaved intelligently. But if from one moment he looks ahead to another, the intelligent man can never be certain of being intelligent, nor of being able to count on that intelligence improperly termed his own. He knows it is not always at the ready like a sword worn on his belt, or as easy to command as his will, that strange psychic mechanism that at least in principle is always ready to ignite in a decision. The operation of the intelligence is enhanced by continual use, by a diet of concentration, by different techniques of special refurbishing, but ultimately it is beyond complete control. Goethe was more than exact when he wrote: "He is right whoever believes he doesn't know how he thinks. When one thinks, everything is a gift." That's it exactly. A felicitous idea appears suddenly in our mind's cavity the way a startled bird enters our window in springtime. This is why the intelligent man, far from being comfortable, is ever haunted by fear of the stupid things he may think; and it is precisely this feeling of always being about to be stupid that is intelligence in the intelligent man; it forces him to live incessantly on the alert so as to avoid making errors, and thus he moves among probable stupidities, like a circus cyclist running a slalom of bottles. The stupid person, on the other hand, is so sure of himself that he doesn't foresee his incipient obtuseness and as a result submerges himself without qualms in seas of stupidity. This led Anatole France to say, with more reason than not, that he was afraid more of crass than of evil people, because the latter sometimes rest from their labors, but the former never do.

It is remarkable and discouraging in equal parts that the Western figure whom we are safest in calling the most intelligent of all Europeans, René Descartes, Lord of Perron, the brilliant founder of Reason, the creator and teacher of our whole modern era and, what is more, of its greatest glory— that is, that treasure, the physico-mathematical sciences— the philosopher for whom man is reason or intelligence (which for the present we take to be the same thing), so much so that according to him man was only man when reasonable or intelligent—this René Descartes insists again and again in his doctrinal works, his letters, and his private notes on the discontinuity, the adventitiousness, the infrequency and casualness of the pulsations of intelligence in man. Let me say parenthetically what a disgrace it is that no study exists in which Descartes's texts on this theme are collected and his curious sense of the unexpectedness and fortuitousness of this power, man's intelligence, explained.

Years ago in Paris a poll was taken of leading French writers to see why each of them wrote. I was with my friend Paul Valéry when the interviewer arrived; when he asked Valéry why he wrote, the latter said: *"par faiblesse"* (out of weakness). Well, if you ask the intelligent man why he is intelligent and he is a pure-blooded intellectual—not a pseudo-intellectual—he is certain to answer: "By chance, my good man."

Naturally, if he is convinced by this bald assertion of unquestionable fact, the intellectual, who will only live with clarity and authenticity, will feel ashamed when the winds of praise blow in his direction. It seems fraudulent and farcical to accept praise for intelligence, which, rather than a property he owns, is an unpredictable occurrence of which he is not the author, for which he is not responsible—something he doesn't have and doesn't exercise, but that happens to him and in him, the way poor land produces crops of golden wheat in summer, or a black cloud's belly suddenly delivers a bolt of lightning. So you see to what extent modesty was not the gymnastics of an orator, but the precondition of an intellectual vocation and praxis. Because if the intellectual doesn't have doubts, if he can't remain in that state of innocence recommended by Plato, cannot keep alive the naïve child within, he will loose his alertness, his wariness of stupid error that is the sustaining vitamin of his perspicaciousness.

And this situation is perfect, ladies and gentlemen, because otherwise, if an intellectual possessed his intelligence the way the beautiful woman *possessed* her beauty, he would be—admit it—absolutely unbearable. Notice, by the way, that because of its psychic or psycho-physiological mechanism, intelligence simply cannot be professionalized. One can be a "doctor" because one can summon a minimum of medical expertise at any time; but if medicine only occurred to the doctor during a few unforeseeable moments in a year, in the guise of a casual and intermittent series of flashes, obviously medicine as a profession would not exist. And this, ladies and gentlemen—the impossibility of professionalizing intelligence—is the cause of that strange feeling we get when we say or hear the word intellectual, for clearly when we say or hear it we all feel a little ashamed. Our minds, in an immediate reaction, reject whatever implications the word carries about professionalizing the intellect. A man can be a tenor by profession, but not an intellectual.

This is why I did not respond fully and without reservation to the generous praise of our director. But there are additional reasons, of even greater import, which have to do not with the functioning of intelligence but with its mission and task, its very content, its work.

For nearly two centuries, or to be exact—because, as we shall see, there are substantive reasons for being especially precise in our chronology—from 1740 to 1929, the Western intellectual enjoyed a higher position in society than at any other previous time in history. Furthermore, during this period, and especially in the second of these centuries, and to a higher degree around 1900, the only two great social forces that actually ruled the West were money and the intellectual. This privileged position in society caused intellectuals to exercise leadership, official or not. It is a fact that in the eighteenth century for the first time in history the intellectual felt a desire to command. You will say that Plato already proclaimed the necessity of one of the following: either philosophers rule, or rulers become philosophers. But, aside from the fact that this famous saying of Plato's is more complicated than it seems, no one believes for a moment that when he wrote the *The Republic,* he meant it seriously. As we know, Plato was not accustomed to speak seriously; instead he spoke Attic, which is a mode of discourse that keeps the sword of seriousness in the sheath of humor. This we call *eironeia,* irony—according to Alphonse Daudet, the most lovely word in the dictionary. If Plato spoke thus, it was not because he really wanted philosophers to rule, but, on the contrary, because he considered it impossible, utopian, paradoxical, irritating. Irony is really the most polite form of provocation. But d'Alembert, the geometer, Diderot, the ideologue, and Rousseau, the dreamer, certainly had a serious desire to command, and they infected intellectuals of subsequent generations with the urge to command. About 1900 a great deal of homage was paid to the type of man who, in place of the ancient sword of a paladin, wielded the new idea, the lucid word, and the pen of style. Remember the etymon of "style" is "writing tip," and tip is the abbreviation of a weapon.

This is no place to give the causes that brought the intellectual such unexpected fortune, but they can be summed up by the fact that during those two centuries the world controlled by European civilization was sustained by a faith in progress, by the belief that humanity had at last joined the convoy called "culture," which would lead it ever onward to better and better modes of existence, and so on. Now then, the creative force behind this progressive culture was reason, intelligence. This explains the social preeminence of the intellectual.

This belief was a gross error, a grotesque *quid pro quo*, and a perversion of intellectual life. By the seventeenth century, the intellectual had already vanquished the clerics and warriors—who had formerly dominated—and suffered from a disease that, as Toynbee has recently shown, overtakes all conquerors and amounts to a historical law he calls "the intoxication of victory"—an idea that we shall need to keep uppermost in our minds. I was amazed at the calmness, naïveté, and blindness of the intellectuals around 1900, and especially in 1920, who believed their situation would last. And I am amazed they didn't even notice the obvious, extreme contrast between their privileged position and the way their kind had been treated by previous history, that is, the fact that the true intellectual, far from being spoiled, has usually been persecuted, beaten, jailed, ridiculed, or at the very least conscientiously ignored. Yet, when I myself reached the stage when the intellectual with a true vocation receives his first flashes of insight—a stage, as we shall see, that can normally be exactly determined—I foresaw that human history once again was about to turn 180 degrees to execute one of those fundamental shifts that characterize it; I saw that the modern era—with the fountain of its inspiration dry, and its principles exhausted—was dying, as I wrote in 1913; and that the idea of progress was a naïve one that revealed a basic insufficiency in our eighteenth-century thought, not yet digested and expelled but fatally stuck in the Western mind (in a moment we shall see, through a rigorous diagnosis, what caused this aberration); in short, it seemed incorrect for intellectuals to accept that privileged position.

Several times prior to 1920, but with the formality of a specific program in "Reform of Intelligence," published in 1925, I warned my fellow philosophers of the fatal step of accepting the praise of a propitious hour, of failing to resist the temptation to command, even though the genius Auguste Comte had already shown in 1840 that for the intellectual, "Toute la participation dans le commandement est radicalement dégradante." And nearly a quarter of a century ago I myself wrote: "The failure of this imperialistic effort of the intelligence is evident. It failed to make man happy and, at the same time, the intelligence lost its powers of inspiration. In order to command, one has to do violence to one's own thought so as to adapt it to the temperament of the masses. Gradually ideas loose their sharpness and transparency and are clouded over with pathos. Nothing causes greater harm to an ideology than trying to convince others of its truth. In being an apostle, a thinker gradually drifts away from his initial doctrine until finally nothing remains but its caricature. With intelligence thus engaged in so improper a task, it ceases to perform its authentic mission: to forge new standards that will replace the old ones as they wane. Here is the reason for the serious crisis today, characterized less by conformity to higher principles than by a complete lack of them. A situation such as this requires that intelligence retreat from social prominence, draw back into itself."

Later, things moved even more quickly, so that earlier predictions have become old history, and even ancient history. And following a dialectic of pure contradiction—which is not, as Hegel and Marx would have it, the characteristic march of all history but only of dull-witted epochs, the atypical ones, where history, reduced to meager participation, virtually becomes pure mechanics, and men are downgraded to inert atoms—intellectuals have gone from being everything to being nothing, from being the pride and glory of nations to being swept off the stage of society, from apparently directing the course of humanity to not even being listened to. The latter is our situation today, and—obviously—I am not alluding to any particular nation but to our entire planet. And if there is some corner where this has not yet happened, this exception must be explained with extreme care, for it is certainly an anomaly.

The pervasiveness of the situation forces us to recognize it openly and to give it an adequate formulation—we must not exclaim over it, but address it with serenity. An adequate expression of these events would be: for years now, before the wars we are immersed in began—I say *wars*, since there is more than one, many in fact, all mixed together in a long confused chain, so long that it reaches to the horizon's edge and beyond . . .—for years now, as I say, a momentous experiment not tried for two thousand five hundred years has been under way in the West (that is, in the whole world) to organize human life without counting on intellectuals at all. Of course, you must realize that anyone who, a quarter of a century ago, wrote what I have just read about intellectuals retreating to solitude to purify and prepare themselves would be unlikely to be surprised or worried on behalf of the intellectual by any attempt to count him out. Still, there is an enormous difference between what I thought then and what is happening now. I urged solitude on the intellectual as the best way of *being* an intellectual—as we shall see—and hence as the most fertile way of collaborating in human life at large, of being some use to mankind. The intellectual must tell others what he discovers in his fruitful solitude; he must broadcast his solitude to mankind from the desert life he has undertaken. The intellectual is above all a *Vox clamantis in deserto*. But there is now an effort to totally suppress the intellectual's collaboration in human life—apparently because people believe, in good faith or bad (notice this strange character of faith, that it is always good or bad), because they believe, as I said, that intellectuals are unnecessary. Someone in Seville sent a local clockmaker a watch that had come apart, and the clockmaker returned the repaired watch a few days later, but with one piece left over because, as he said, the piece was unnecessary. It seems, then, that people all over the world similarly believe that the intellectual is to the clock of the West what the leftover part was to the clockmaker from Seville. Yet I observe this dangerous experiment with interest and equanimity. The intellectual acknowledges at the outset that anything is possible, even what is most improbable; one must examine each case to see that things are actually that way. Being an intellectual means living with doubt and in doubt, being at sea without surrendering to seasickness or dizziness; a life in continual danger of drowning, where there is no alternative but to swim to stay afloat. Yet an intellectual prefers this vocation and its risk to the easy calm of an atrophied belief. This immersion in doubt is neither caprice, nor whim, nor obsession, nor a longing for ambiguities—which would be pathological—it is just the opposite, and to such an extent that we can further define the intellectual as fundamentally determined that he will stop doubting and will achieve certainty. Still, it is obvious that in order to stop doubting one must first have been in doubt!

We have thus raised and considered the question of whether the intellectual has a special and necessary place in the great adventure-enterprise of human life, or whether, on the contrary, he is a fifth wheel, something that can and should be dispensed with. This does not mean that the question will be particularly important in these lectures. But they all deal with it implicitly in the search for an answer. Still, only in this lecture is it dealt with directly and not hereafter; so that now, momentarily, the question of the intellectual is before us. Our discussion does not turn on the poet or the technician, varieties of the human that have existed from time immemorial and have a clearly drawn profile. Nor do we speak of the scientists or refer to the specific sciences, which, strictly speaking, are the only ones there are. As a historical phenomenon, scientists are much more recent than poets and technicians, but as with the latter, people have always been convinced they were necessary to provide well-being or relieve pain, to invent aspirin or create a play, to discover the elevator and the telephone. Rather, I refer here to a strange variety of man whose condition has never been clearly defined, who fits none of the above categories, and who, since his existence has always been associated with vague, imprecise, mistaken, silly names—such as "thinker," or "intellectual," the one I have chosen because it reproduces in modern languages nearly identical ambiguities, lack of precision, petulance, and ridiculousness that the words *sophós, sophistés, philósophos* came to have for the Greeks.

The only clear thing to be said at present about this enigmatic figure is that the intellectual is involved in generating opinions regarding the important themes that concern mankind; he is an opinion-giver. His occupation is more than strange since everyone has opinions. And that is why there is no language without an expression such as "It is general opinion that. . . ." This is to say that "everybody" and "anybody" form a gigantic person who already has an opinion. This makes it even more peculiar that certain individuals want to make of the universal occupation of opinion-giving a personal, untransferable vocation and profession. Some time ago this led me to pose myself the following question, which, although it seems unlikely, had at that time never been thematically addressed: where, when, why, and how did the exorbitant fauna of the intellectual appear in history? What is the intellectual's mission, his destiny, and his role? For what purpose *are they there?* Our general inabil-

ity to see genuinely human phenomena in a historical perspective—which is the only adequate one, that is, as having
appeared one fine day and destined to disappear on some
future day, instead of as something always there—this attitude has kept the obvious hidden from view: that the human
type called "intellectual" is a mere historical contingency
that blossomed in a very restricted region of our planet at a
very precise date. It happened in the Eastern Mediterranean
region, and—by an unusual coincidence—at the same time
in two worlds and civilizations not yet in touch, distinct,
that is: the Syrian world on the one hand, and the Hellenic
world on the other, around the year 700 B.C. At one and the
same time the prototype of the intellectual appeared in Greece
with Hesiod and in the land of the Hebrews with Amos,
the first prophet. The prophets were the intellectuals of Israel.
And Hesiod is soon followed by the *sophoi*, the thinkers, the
wisemen—canonized in the Platonic school as the "seven."
The "seven wisemen" were enormously suggestive figures
who inaugurated the great, thousand-year-old dance of
thought, like a corps de ballet, at the same time striking and
gauche: exceptional figures, in short, about whom there is
naturally not a single notable book and to whom we shall
have to return later to say something that ought to have
been said but never was. In rapid succession the first scientists spring to life: the physiologists and the mysterious
Pythagoras, with his inestimable influence, and Parmenides
and Heraclitus, the two founders of philosophy, strictly
speaking, the two gigantic dinosaurs of the fauna intellectual. What role are these unexpected creatures to play, these
enigmatic characters about whom we know only that they
said clever or paradoxical things, and that no sooner did
they appear than they produced a tension on the skin of
history—a tension and a prickling that are the unmistakable
effect of intellectual labor—and have scarcely ever stopped
these two thousand six hundred years past. In order fully

to understand a human mode, however important, it is imperative to observe it at the moment it appears, in its cradle, at its hour of birth—*in statu nascente*, when it is still in a pure state and the undergrowth has not yet begun to cover and choke it.

The birth of the fauna intellectual is of capital importance in order to see just what that curiosity called "philosophy" is. We have to spend an entire lecture on this subject since— an extraordinary fact!—this important subject has never been treated with precision, without evasive generalities, and in a direct way. But now we need only look at one facet of the affair: the one that reveals the mission of the intellectual, or why the universe includes those extravagant beings we intellectuals are.

Amos was the first prophet in our sense of the word, which was preserved and transmitted to us by Christianity. The human mode initiated by Amos will be venerated, respected, and repeated by all subsequent prophets. In him we have the first profile of the prophet and its purest example. "Prophet," however, does not mean, as is commonly thought, one who speaks of the future, foretelling what is to come. Undoubtedly the words of the prophets contained antici- pations of future events, predictions—yet remember it is similarly a function of the laws of physics to foresee the exact outcome of future events. The laws of physics, how- ever, make no pretense, apparently, of foretelling but are solely dedicated to *telling* the truth about what things *are;* and, as it seems, when one has the truth about what a thing is, one also has the exact design of its future behavior. Here let me stress two points. First, there seems to be a secret or as yet unclear connection between *telling* the truth about a thing's being and *foretelling* the future; so much so that both telling and foretelling seem coextensive. Second, while in the intellectual of Greek origin, whose lineal descendant we are, foretelling seemingly took the form of a pure and unemotional telling, with the foretelling part disguised, in the intellectual of Syrian origin, in the prophet, telling is normally offered in the burning and dramatic guise of foretelling, prediction—because the word of the prophet, since it is seen as proceeding from heaven where God resides, unwittingly imitates the turbulent style of the tempest, reaching us with thunder and lightning, in short, in apocalyptic form. Thus, while the man from Greece calls his formal telling, discourse, or *Logos*, the prophet calls his revelation, or *apocalypsis*. When, later in the course, we seek the reason for this difference, it will reveal unexpected depths to the great metaphysical problem: the problem of being.

The Septuagint—those Hellenized Jews who lived in the third and second centuries B.C., translated the Old Testament, and were supposed to be seventy in number—searched for a Greek word for the Hebrew *Nabi*, and *prophetes* seemed the best choice. *Nabi* was a very old word in Hebrew, older than Hebrew itself, which proceeded from some unknown and distinct source. This ought not to surprise us, because its oldest meaning is one of the most ancient human realities and persists today among peoples we used to call savage and to whom we now apply the very English, very courteous and euphemistic name, "primitive." The translation was excellent, but another time, since today we must hurry on, you will see that this matter is more complicated than it at first appears. We know translating from one language to a very different one, above all when they express widely divergent cultures, is a hopeless, utopian task. In vain we assume that a word in one language has its double or twin in the other, another word that means the same thing. This would require, at the hour of birth of both languages, an unlikely parallelism to have existed between them, which would itself count for little inasmuch as words, like all human creations, are never still, but always changing sound and meaning, having adventures.

And in this regard I will say in public what I said privately to a certain Portuguese philologist—his friendship does me honor—in case it may interest anyone here as a subject for study: there is a fascination in studying the divergent semantic evolution, that is, the parallel biographies, of a series of words that Portuguese and Spanish share. There would be no better way to obtain exactly the different outlines of our collective souls. Thus, I suspect, although I cannot be certain, that one would soon discover a clear tendency in Portuguese to attract the pejorative meaning of a word, and this to a greater degree than is normal in other languages, which would be symptomatic of a certain collective pessimism. For example, while the word *"azar"* in Spanish still means any kind of fortune, whether good or bad, its Portuguese twin only means adverse fortune, misfortune, misadventure, bad luck. Similarly, *"exquisito"* traditionally meant whatever was select, set apart, whether good or bad, what for one reason or another stands above the common or usual. Now, we could say this word has done well in Spanish, has prospered and now means what is excellent, the very best, the cream of the cream, just like the French *"exquis,"* whereas in Portuguese, this word has fared badly and today it means what stands out for opposite reasons—the extravagant, wrong, difficult, almost monstrous, and so forth.

Nabi means the possessed, the exalted, the seer, the lunatic, the ecstatic, and since ecstasy means, in its turn, beside oneself, *nabi* means a man beside himself, a frenetic man.

Among a vast portion of today's primitive peoples, we find men whose office or occupation is to be beside themselves, to become frenzied at specified times by means of the most varied and, at times, difficult techniques. Sometimes it is through an orgiastic dance that produces dizziness, causing the dancer to fall into an ecstatic trance. In other cases, the method involves drinking alcohol or chewing hallucinogenic substances. Still others pass the night in

the temples of their Gods, where scents and essences produce those vivid dreams the Romans called *incubatio*. The
goal of all these techniques is to extinguish man's normal
mental states and to provoke abnormal ones such as dreams
and even hallucinations. The point is to stop seeing what is
around one and see visions instead. Now, these frenzied or
visionary men are awarded a preeminent place in the societies to which they belong, often the most important of all.
Their *exquisite* work—the Portuguese word is perfect here—
their *exquisite* labor of going mad, of getting drunk or drugged
is neither caprice nor private vice, but a public service, a
mediation the society needs.

Man exercises two different sets of mental activities: one
consists in seeing, hearing, touching, and so forth, or sense
perceptions. Of course, thanks to the incredible weight of
an archaic psychology, most people believe we only have
five senses, when in fact there are eleven. I can't take time
now to explain the other six. These sense perceptions give
us the things around us, whose use or resistance makes up
the greater part of our lives. These perceptions stimulate
the activity of our intellect, which compares, distinguishes,
and identifies them so as to form clear ideas in their regard:
what we call concepts, notions, reasons. This is our intellectual set of mental activities.

But beside our perceptions and concepts or intellectuali-
zations, which are quite ordinary, usual, and common in
their regularity, man experiences other mental activities that,
from the way they arise, by the infrequency of their functioning, are exceptional. Such are the states of drunkenness,
delirium, trance, and exaltation, but especially, and for the
moment, dreaming. When man sleeps and the world of
familiar things disappears, he confronts a world of things
unlike his waking experience but no less vivid. Asleep, man
sees and touches strange beings, monsters he never saw when
awake, human and semi-human figures with strange powers

and appearances; he witnesses scenes where the laws of daily
life do not hold. There appear, or rather reappear—and this
has had a decisive influence on human history—dead ances-
tors who live again, who speak to him, offer him counsel,
threaten or promise him things. As in dreams, so with
drunken visions, drugged states of mind, ecstatic trances.

Each group of mental activities offers a different kind of
reality, two distinct worlds that, in principle, has an equal
right to be considered real. How does man deal with this
duality? To which set does he give greater credence? On
which does he depend more? And, in like manner, which
of the different worlds will seem decisive, more important
and authentic, that is, real?

For us the dilemma has been decided. We firmly believe
that the clear perceptions and the clear ideas formed about
them by our intellect are the only certain means of arriving
at reality, discovering it, and orienting us in it. In other
words, we have decided in favor of the intellectual method
of clear, rational or logical thinking.

On the basis of our present conviction we disqualify the
supposed realities that appear in dreams, hallucinations,
trances, and ecstatic states, in deliriums and drunkenness.
All this, we say, is unreal; the things that appear to us in
these exceptional states are not real things but subjective
creations belonging to another faculty in man—marvellous
but mistaken and uncontrolled—called fantasy. In dreams,
in drunkenness, and in deliriums, there are no real things
but fantastic imaginings or phantoms. By contrast with our
set of intellectual faculties, then, this set is fantastical,
visionary, or mystical thought.

But the intellectual method is a fairly recent discovery in
human history. It occurred about two thousand five hundred
years ago, a rather short span compared with the million
years, according to well-founded, geological discoveries based
particularly on the study of glaciers, since our species, *homo*

sapiens, appeared on earth. That discovery is contemporary with the appearance of the first intellectuals, who were the ones—obviously!—who made the discovery and, therefore, deserve, strictly speaking, the name. But before them, for tens of thousands of years, primitive man was unaware he possessed an intellect, although he worked with it, used concepts constantly, and was logical in his thinking—albeit in the same way the *bourgeois gentilhomme* spoke prose, without realizing it. Lévy-Bruhl's idea that a prelogical man preceded rational man is erroneous, asinine; and I allow myself this crude expression because one day we shall delve as deeply as possible into the primitive mind and then we will treat that industrious author's thesis in detail. The only true part of his argument is the indubitable fact that primitive man did not consider his intellect—since he was unaware of its existence—a method for discovering true reality; on the contrary, he believed it was visionary thought that revealed true reality. Dreams and deliriums were man's first teachers. They were the source of certain fundamental ideas on which his concept of reality was based; in spite of what is usually thought, ideas that are still active at the deepest level of our present thinking have their origin here. That strange and extraordinary world of visions, dreams, alcohol, and orgies seemed to him the deepest, most authentic reality, inhabited by decisive powers that ruled visible things and, above all, human destiny. Since that visionary world was uncertain of access, it seemed mysterious in character and, as such, assumed the qualities of what would later be called the divine. Because of the foreignness of its forms and scenes, this mystery inspired terror, it was tremendous, in the most literal sense of the word; it was the *mysterium tremendum*, but, for all that, it attracted man because of its very foreignness; it was fascinating, *mysterium fascinans*, and these two inseparable qualities, terror and fascination, were characteristic of the holy in the truest sense. When, in later centuries,

the word "holy" was applied to certain virtuous men canonized by the Church, the word lost the ultra-terrestrial and
frightening splendor it had had in Latin; but that meaning
survives in Church formulas, such as the antiphony to God
that says: *"Tu solus Santus, tu solus Altissimus,* or as St.
Augustine expressed his feeling of closeness to God, saying:
"Et inhorresco et inardesco" (You terrify me and beguile me;
you frighten and enchant me).

And just as once the intellectual method was established,
books were written and academies and universities and laboratories and highly refined techniques evolved to make use
of the clear perceptions and the derivation of strict or rational
concepts, so primitive man, who exists still and makes up
the majority in civilized countries, created visionary techniques and methodically cultivated his deliriums.*

---

* Due to a lack of time, the lecture, reproduced here according to the draft
Ortega prepared, was shortened. This is why a paragraph and a sentence
or so are repeated in the second lecture. According to the account in *O
Século* (December 21, 1944), the last sentence of this first lecture was, "And
in this way human thought began." [Ed.]

2

Existence and consistency. To be and to have
been. Explaining a past philosophy and doing
philosophy. Doing philosophy is the only philosophy. The antiquity of the visionary method.
Fantasy and rationality. The enigma of the visible. World and transworld. Delirium and reason.
Amos, the interpreter. Intellectual solitude. The
prophet in opposition: an opinion against public
opinion. The intellectual as bearer of a truth not
exclusively his. The locus of truth; resistance to
truth. The mission of the intellectual: to oppose
and seduce.

I WAS INVITED to give a philosophy course in this Faculty
and I assume this obligation in the strictest sense, that is, as
demanding a maximum effort on my part. This means I am
formally obligated to explain the fundamental problems of
philosophy, in the most precise and rigorous form those
problems permit and our present understanding allows. This
does not necessarily mean that this most rigorous possible
form of philosophical explanation will be the one some of
you expect; some of you may have certain expectations
because you mistakenly think you know what philosophy
is. Don't attribute what I said to vanity or presumption on
my part. I don't mean I am certain I can give such an explanation; I am only giving formal expression to my under-

standing of my obligation, my contract, which is that I must expound a philosophy that *is* philosophy.

But this proposition—a philosophy that is philosophy—has a double meaning as do all judgments or sentences employing the verb *to be*, because this fearsome verb, with its slender shape and inexhaustible content—where the best minds of the last two thousand years have been chipping away like stonecutters at an infinitely rich vein of ore—has, like the duck-and-rabbit illusion, two basically different meanings that unceasingly exchange places before our eyes, dizzying our understanding.

When we say, "The swan is," we mean the swan exists, that there are swans. This is the existential meaning of the verb *to be*. But if we say, "The centaur is a lover of nymphs," we don't mean that the centaur exists or that there are centaurs—but only that if centaurs did exist or there were centaurs, inevitably they would be lovers of nymphs; that this characteristic, propensity, or habit belongs to the entity "centaur," whether they exist or not; that we cannot think "centaur" and not think it with a human torso and equine flanks, with Pan's pipes at its lips, and with that insolent desire for nymphs. Rather than saying that there are centaurs, we say they are thus and so, that this is their essence. This is the predicative or essential meaning of *to be*. But since the word "essence," an erudite and violent translation of the fresh, ordinary Greek word *ousía*, reality, comes to us burdened with the weight of two thousand years of philosophical theory, I like to replace it with another more common and vivacious term.

Here we have our first example of a deliberate and by now customary tendency—you will soon see what real and productive reasons there are for it—to replace the vocabulary of an old, dried-up terminology with the most common and, at times, most vernacular, metaphorical, colloquial, and homely of expressions. Until now, in the manner of the scholastics, it was usual to juxtapose the terms "existence" and "essence," the fact that something *is* with the *way* that it is. Instead, I like to say that an object exists or not, and, in addition, that every object has this or that *consistency;* so that I juxtapose existence and consistency. One could discuss the existence or consistency of any object we might mention. Thus I replace the traditional "essence" with the simpler, more ordinary "consistency." And we have only to distinguish between two senses of the verb *to be*—existing and consisting of—to realize there are curious objects that, while not existing in a complete, normal sense, nevertheless have a consistency independent of our wishes and do not depend on our attributing certain properties to them. A mathematical triangle does not really exist; nevertheless, we know the sum of its angles always equals two right angles. This is part of its consistency. Although it is incomprehensible that anything should have qualities, properties, habits and still not exist in the fullest sense of existing, we now must face the likelihood of there being more tenuous, less "complete" modes of existence than those that pertain with real things, and that inevitably, in however tenuous a sense, triangles must exist. We call this tenuous and problematic mode of existence *ideal existence,* and today in mathematics one of the most important theorems is the theorem of existence, which says whether a certain number or magnitude exists. Ideal existence is what the scholastics called *ens rationis.* Suárez, in fact, had an extremely original doctrine about the *ens rationis* that decisively influenced Leibnitz. (He is the same great Jesuit Suárez with whom our kind director tried to compare me in a flight of benevolence when he first introduced me.) Now, the same must be said of the centaur, although admittedly it does not exist the way the Percheron does. Since it is at least possessed of the well-known and suggestive consistency created for it in mythology—and, hence, has attributes not dependent on our wishes—the centaur must possess some mode of existence, since with no effort on our part we can evoke a centauric horse from blackest nothingness and have it gallop through an unreal spring breeze, over emerald fields, with its mane and tail flying, in pursuit of white nymphs.

Whether it is valid or not to talk of an ideal existence, the crucial point is that the true and positive existential meaning of the term "being" is actual, real, or complete existence. But having established this fact, which—as you see—is quite simple, yet also fundamental, and will be especially useful later on in numerous ways, let us return to the point that called it forth.

I said my obligation—in the most binding sense this can have for me—entailed the exposition of a body of thought that is properly philosophical. But this means two things. First, I must provide the most rigorous possible theory for the most essential problems commonly considered philosophical, that is, make certain that this theory is philosophy—to speak of its consistency. But second, I must also set forth a philosophy that still *is* today the philosophy it consists of. You will presently have no doubt about the difference. If I only undertook to offer a philosophy that *was*, I would be meeting my obligation in too easy and limited a way. For a philosophy that *was*, *is* no longer; while it retains the consistency proper to all philosophy, in the other sense it is not philosophy; it no longer exists. As far as our present interests are concerned, there are only two modes of existence: God's eternal existence—to use this concept in its strictest philosophical sense—or momentary existence. Either something exists eternally and is divine, or it exists in the moment and is, now and only now. What was, no longer is, or, to use another formula, we can say that it *is* in the form of having been. And at once we realize that this mode of *is*—as having been—is, like the modes of the centaur and the triangle, not a complete or full but a deficient sort of being, a less-than-total mode of existence, very close to non-being, non-existence. Furthermore, even the iota of being these modes have is not their own. What was, is called the past. Notice the mistake in our expression that something *is* past—because if something *is past*, it isn't at all—its being has passed over into non-being. A pain that is past no longer hurts; when love is gone it no longer moves us, injures us. But we do remember the past, have it with us, or we make it part of our present again, which amounts to the same thing; we *re-present* it by injecting it with a little of our present's existential lifeblood, a little of its being. The past can only be, only exist when afixed to our present, our now. This makes the past one of the two dimensions of the present; the other is the future. *Being-no-longer* and *not-being-yet* are equally *non-being*, since they live off what *is-now*.

This is why to speak with precision about something that was, we ought to say that it is not presently what "is," but only *re-presently* so, since it has been *re-called*. This is why I said that any philosophy that *was, is not* a philosophy.

Nothing would be easier or more comfortable than to offer a philosophy that was. (In truth there has never been a really difficult philosophy.) We could do it together, effortlessly—half asleep, at siesta time, or at breakfast while reading the newspaper, or with feet up and head back while we listen to the melancholy unfolding of the melodic skein of a *fado*.

This would be easy, dear friends—because since such a philosophy was, it is already there, all of it, stiff and still, like a folded umbrella. We have only to tuck it under our arm and walk off.

But a philosophy that *is*, such as the one in which you and I must engage, is not simply there; what it is hasn't yet come into being. It is becoming, happening in us, we are in the process of becoming *it*. It is not outside, but being produced within us. So that, properly speaking, it isn't philosophy but a philosophizing—you and I doing philosophy, being philosophy.

This is worth the effort. But will require a lot of effort. The noun "philosophy" is an abstraction like any other noun—whereas we must make it an authentically real verb. In this course of lectures we will move in an active, verbal way; if God and chance permit, we will *be* philosophy. Everyone according to his lights, but if you pay attention, even the least little bit, you should manage to "become" philosophy for one hour a week. Even if I seem the author of this particular philosophy and you its recipients, this is not a significant difference, for the simple reason that if I am "more philosophy" than you are, since I am by no means all of philosophy and no one comes near being all of it, there is only—solely—a matter of degree, an evanescent difference between us that counts for little. You may think this mere courtesy on my part, a compliment paid, but you would be wrong; the fact is that I don't have time to explain how much more sincere I am than you may think.

In order for a philosophy to be truly of the present, it has to be intimately connected with what philosophy was. This is not open to question; philosophy must absorb past philosophy, assimilate it. We too will be concerned with past philosophy, and on some points in a stricter sense than heretofore. But notice that in saying we have absorbed and assimilated something, we are saying we have made it disappear. I even doubt that there is a more complete way of making something disappear than by absorbing and assimilating it. This strange phenomenon, the core of the historical process wherein all new eras conserve and at the same time destroy a previous era, constitutes, according to Hegel, the most important category of Mind, for him the absolute reality. This process he calls *Aufhebung*, a hard word to translate into our Iberian languages, but one that years ago

I proposed to replace with our *absorber*, since to absorb is at once to conserve and to destroy: to cause what is there to disappear—*Verschwinden*, in Hegel's terms—and, at the same time, to integrate it into ourselves. In shape and outline a second love is always different from the first, precisely because it follows the first, is relative to it, and we have the first always before us. So that the new love begins by being cruel to the first one—killing it—but at the same time is forced to retain it within, shelter it, and, to a degree, perpetuate it. This is even clearer in the case of man's ideas. A new idea is formed in view of the old one, whose defects it avoids and bypasses; but this means the new idea has the old one inside it, thanks to which it was engendered. This is why many, many years ago it occurred to me to say that while in nature mothers bear offspring in their wombs, in history the female offspring that are new ideas bear their own mothers in their wombs.*

. . .

Among a vast portion of today's primitive peoples, we find men whose office or occupation is to be beside themselves, to become frenzied at specific times by means of the most varied and, at times, difficult techniques. Sometimes through an orgiastic dance that produces dizziness, causing the dancer to fall into an ecstatic trance. In other cases, the method involves drinking alcohol or chewing hallucinogenic substances. Still others pass the night in the temples of their Gods, where scents and essences produce those vivid dreams the Romans called *incubatio*. The goal of all these techniques is to extinguish man's normal mental states and to provoke abnormal ones such as dreams and even hallucinations. The point is to stop seeing what is around one and see visions instead. Now, these frenzied or visionary men are awarded

---

*The pages are missing that contained the transition from these preliminary considerations of the *second* lecture and the continuation of the subject treated at the close of the *first* lecture. [Ed.]

a preeminent place in the societies to which they belong, often the most important of all. Their *exquisite* work—the Portuguese word is perfect here—their *exquisite* labor of going mad, of getting drunk or drugged is neither caprice nor private vice, but a public service, a mediation the society needs.

Such people existed when the primitive mind was still unaware of the intellectual method, which appeared barely twenty-five hundred years ago; it was discovered by certain men who, as a consequence, logically deserve to be called intellectuals. This intellectual method, or clear, rational, logical thought has seemed ever since, to certain Western minorities, the only sure means of knowing true reality, discovering it, and finding one's way in it. But the primitive mentality, which persists in the majority of the inhabitants of the civilized nations, believed that dreams, drunkenness, delirium, and trance, put us in touch with true reality. From our point of view, these mental activities unleash fantasy, that other human power, and what is revealed is never reality but the phantoms, the phantasmagoria that it produces. Instead of the intellectual method, primitive man has always preferred the method we call fantastical or visionary. For this reason he developed techniques for delirium so as to have vivid dreams, get drunk, and fall into a trancelike state. This explains the surprising fact that drugs are among the most ancient inventions of mankind; what is more, since ancient times man has known nearly all the natural drugs, and very little was left to be discovered later. There only remained the extraction and distillation of certain alkaloids; but opium, Indian hemp, Jimson weed, and alcohol have been used by men since the dawn of history. Drinking wine and cultivating grapes, while more recent, have similar half-magic, half-religious origins. The expression *in vino veritas*, which has a leering, in-group meaning now, is an old Latin saying with an entirely religious significance: truth comes to us in the exaltation of drunkenness. This is why we find an exact equivalent in the Greek expression, *oinos kaí aléth-era*—wine is truth—a prayer of the Dionysian cult; it explains why when Plato at eighty wrote his *Laws (Nómoi)*, he felt he should devote one of its books to a discussion of the extent to which wine served pedagogical, religious, and social ends. But to go back even farther, before drugs were discovered, in the Paleolithic Age, the first about which we possess a kind of historical—or prehistorical—knowledge, mankind had already found a way to become intentionally frenzied, or beside himself. In fact, corresponding data from prehistory and ethnography indicate that the first cave or cavern used by man, and the first huts he built, were not dwellings for daily life but were very likely what ethnographers call "houses to transpire in." Certain plants were burned in caves, and the smoke made the inhabitants loose their reason and fall to raving. Or else, they brought in red-hot stones, and the heat in such a confined space would make them sweat until a trance resulted. It is interesting that man, who is known as a rational animal, first used his reason in an attempt to loose it—which, since this seems rather extreme, is grounds for the suspicion that man wasn't at first very rational. It is not even clear why we think him so today.

But it would be a flagrant mistake, friends, if proud and self-satisfied at being the *nouveaux riches* of reason, we looked down on the primitive mind's visionary method, however useless and childish it may seem, and failed to notice the more important point that primitive man and the masses today both long for visions. Because this would mean that neither was content with what they saw, heard, or touched, that is, with what they perceive through sense perception.

We have only to press with a shadow of our attention on the fact that primitive man needs to see visions, become a visionary, in order to make this simple but important discovery: primitive man, like later man, or everyman, when faced with the immediacy of things and on finding himself submerged for life in a world made up of them, that is, in the visible world—the one we call "this" world—finds it deficient, wanting: not by accident, but because that world is made up of an infinite number of mere unconnected facts, of this happening, then that happening, and then that, and so on forever in an overwhelming rush in which he feels lost. Thus, what the visible world presents is an enigma, and this is why it seems deficient: it is the oppressive presence of an infinite problem and a multiform mystery. What is visible is the enigma of it, like the strokes of a hieroglyphic that are there precisely to announce that they have no meaning in themselves, but hide it, that the meaning is behind them and must be teased out. So the world we live in appears as an immense and disquieting enigma, which, like any mask, both announces and hides another decisive reality lying behind it, that is, the face behind the mask—a reality in essence latent, not visible, but by nature secret and arcane. Usually, we try to distract ourselves from the uneasiness this causes, desiring to forget that by only living in this visible, immediate world, we are not "in the truth, that instead we inhabit a fraud, a deception, an error—life is one great masquerade, a continual, involuntary carnival. This is why primitive man, later man, and everyman longs to breach the deceiving curtain of this world, to enlarge its natural opening in order to see what lies beyond, that is, to see a world that is in essence different from this one. And here is a theme that will concern us throughout these lectures—man in two worlds at the same time: the insufficient, visible one and the virtual one he longs for. The world and the world beyond. It is an age-old dispute as to which method best guarantees us access to the world beyond. The visionaries say delirium; the intellectuals say reason or intelligence.

Prior to the eighth century, when Amos was born, there were *nebiîm* (singular: *nabi*) in Israel—visionaries, ecstatic or frenzied persons. There were a great many of them. Their job was popular because they oversaw traditional or ingrained beliefs and guarded public opinion. They practiced orgiastic rituals, got drunk, became intoxicated—all at public expense. They received a salary. (When a man performs an activity professionally there is no reason to suppose he has a marked vocation for it. Profession and vocation sometimes coincide but have nothing to do with one another. Since there is more to this than meets the eye, we must examine it some day.) These professionals of delirium were often sly and corruptible but they were always popular. Balaam and his prophetic ass is a good example: he is a semi-burlesque figure in Hebrew folklore.

Now then, the Greek word *Prophetes* did not mean a visionary, an exalted or delirious person, but quite the opposite. *Prophetes* were men assigned to temples from which oracles issued—at Delphi, at Dodona—and their mission was interpretation, that is, clarifying and declaring the words and murmurings (by themselves all but unintelligible) of the priestess or sibyl when she was in a trance. As we know, in order to give answers the sibyl and the priestess climbed on a tripod. This was because the sibyl had to be directly over a hole or opening in the earth—the one at Delphi still exists—beneath which flowed a subterranean fountain of mineral water charged with fetid gases to intoxicate her. This hole through which divine inspiration, the word of God, came was like a small mouth; since *os, oris* is mouth in Latin, its diminutive would be *oraculum*. Strictly speaking, then, the oracle is the small orifice or rift in the earth through which primitive subterranean divinities spoke, mouthing things to man.

Thus the *prophetes* was neither a delirious person nor a visionary; on the contrary, he was a clear-headed person who, with his good sense, gave meaning to the unintelligible oracle and, as it were, rationalized it. Certainly, the *prophetes* did not speak for himself but transmitted the divine message; he did this, interpreted and transmitted the message, on his own, however, with his clear, lucid mind. Now then, the kind of prophet that begins with Amos is the irreconcilable enemy of all visionaries, orgiasts, and ravers. This explains what must seem simply incomprehensible to the average reader of the Bible: that Amos, and nearly all other prophets in a strict sense, repeat again and again that they are not prophets, in the sense of *nabi* or *nebiîm*, not people who earn a living by becoming delirious, drunk, and pandering to the established beliefs of ancient Israel, the polytheistic belief in gods or Baalim, and the moral disorders this occasions.

So Amos gives us a summary of his biography when in Amos, chapter VII, verse 7, he says: "I am no prophet nor am I a prophet's son; I am a herder of goats and sheep and I also earn a living as a dresser of sycamore-figs."

"Son of a prophet" was the name for associations or groups of *nebiîm*, of delirious people, who were under the protection of some authority or other. Recall that according to the Second Book of Kings, Queen Jezebel kept 850 of these pseudo-prophets at her expense. But what surprises in these verses is that someone in the eighth century B.C. should speak out individually and reveal his autobiography—so there would be no doubt as to the authorship of his sayings or how the sayer lived. We find exactly the same thing a few years later with Hesiod. Just to balance the books!

So that if Amos is no prophet in the traditional, popular sense, in what new sense is he one? What is his view of his role, his mission, his vocation? He himself says laconically in the next verse, which I will subdivide in my commentary: "But the Lord took me apart as I followed the flock"— that is, God removed him from his customary tasks, from usual commerce with the world, with other men, in short, from where he primarily and innocently dwelt. Which means

that he was bereft of others, of *his* world—and was therefore
alone—and then, when he was truly and radically alone, a
fountain of truth sprang from the depths of that solitude.
For the Israelite, the truth comes from God—is the word of
God—for the Greeks, the truth is the rationale of things,
the very being of things. As concerns our present subject,
the source of truth is unimportant, because in either case
man only comes to the truth when by himself; yet there is
nothing vague or mysterious about this, for the simple reason that no one has ever been able to really think, that is,
truly think and to think with truth even so trivial a thing as
two and two are four without being by themselves, with-
drawn, just for an instant, and clearly imagining, evidentially, what two is and what two more is, and what four is.
Usually we do this without really thinking it, that is,
mechanically, blindly—and not evidentially—relying on our
social milieu, since there appear to be certain men called
mathematicians who assure us this is the case. Our usual
thinking that two and two are four is simply a check we
draw on the mathematicians' bank.

So that when man is by himself, in total solitude, in des-
olate solitude and, therefore, alone, without even being there
himself (for the strange thing about authentic solitude is that
we ourselves are the first thing to disappear—the self one
imagined one was), then, as I say, the solitude becomes what
Saint John of the Cross calls, so beautifully, a "sonorous
solitude." Just so, for then things begin to speak their truth
in man—begin to unveil to us what they truly are. In society, in company, in our habitual chores, things are there to
be used and abused or else to abuse us—but we are not
vouchsafed their being, their truth. Things by themselves
cannot reveal their being, which is only made manifest in
speech, in words; they have no voice, but are mute masks
or, if you prefer, have silent, taciturn voices that only the
man who retires from the world and abandons himself can
hear. Then this world of things proffers its silent voice to

the solitary man—whether prophet, thinker, philosopher, or intellectual—"throws" its taciturn voice the way the ventriloquist does through the papier-mâché figure he holds up to the audience. It is not, properly speaking, the thinker who thinks and speaks, but the things themselves that think through him, speaking about themselves. Intelligence, my friends, is essentially a ventriloquist's act. This is what the Greeks understood by *lógos*, *legem*, "saying."

Now let us return to the text: "But the Lord took me apart as I followed the flock and said to me: 'Amos, go and prophesy *against* my people Israel.' "

Notice that the Israel that Jehovah calls his nation or people is also, at the same time, Amos's nation, even though the possessive in each case has the opposite meaning. Israel is God's nation because it belongs to God—but Israel is Amos's nation because Amos belongs to the nation of Israel. Everyone, willingly or not, belongs to some nation. There is no general or abstract man; to be man is to be man according to the mode or manner created thousands of years ago by a collectivity. Amos consists in a substance called Israel—that is why, in every sense of the word, he is an Israelite. Israel is, in like manner, Amos's nation.

We are not adding a thing to Amos's words, but taking something away from them if we change his text to read: "Jehovah, speaking to me, said: 'Go and prophesy *against* your nation.' "

Now then, this is very different from being a *nabi*, the guardian of, and spokesman for, a nation's established ideas, or keeper of its public opinion. It seems we have a new and more authentic way of being a prophet that is the opposite of the traditional way: the new prophet is essentially a prophet *against*.

If now we seek a corresponding phenomenon among the first intellectuals of Greece, we discover that the earliest surviving fragments by the first recorded thinker—that is, Hecate of Milletus, who was later than Thales but before

all the others—begin this way: "The views of the Greeks
are many and ridiculous, but *I*, Hecate, declare the following reasons."

Here God is no more; in his stead there is reason, but the
situation is basically the same. In the present case, man as
an individual sets himself against public opinion. With that
energy and starkness with which, as I said before, human
affairs first see the light of day, we learn that intelligence is
the opinion that opposes public opinion. And it is simply to
acknowledge what this means to say that the destiny of the
intellectual is to be . . . unpopular. Not through choice, or
whim, or chance, but because of the make-up of his vocation and his task; the intellectual must be unpopular,
unpopular with any and every people, whether high or low.
His mission is to correct public opinion by leading them out
of error and gathering them to the truth they require. Since
the Greek for established or public opinion is *doxa*, the intellectual's opinion—always counter-opinion—must be paradox. And in truth, as we shall see, the history of philosophy
is an uninterrupted series of paradoxes.

There is nothing strange about the fact that both the
prophets and the first thinkers of Greece, not to mention
nearly all those that followed, should have suffered perse-
cution. Nor would it make sense for them to complain about
it—the unpopularity of the vocation brings down persecu-
tion on whoever practices it. The true mission of the intellectual is neither to praise nor flatter, but to oppose and
rectify; make straight in the desert a highway for our God,
as Isaiah said [XL,3]. Such a destiny is harsh, difficult, and
terrible—inasmuch as it is one of the rarest examples of the
most authentic manliness. And with few exceptions in his
favor, the intellectual has always been that man Josephus
spoke about. . . .*

*The text from Josephus is missing from the transcript. [Ed.]

Can you wonder, my friends, that anyone who feels this way should hesitate before accepting generous introductory praise?

However, I must insert two warnings here so that all the above will be perfectly clear. First, it would be unjustifiable, pointless insanity for one man to pit his individual opinion against the great monolith of public opinion. There is no reason to suppose that any private opinion would be more valid than that of the many, the public at large. In fact, an intellectual's opinion is valid precisely because it is not his private opinion. The theorem of the geometer, the Theory of Relativity discovered by Einstein, are not theirs alone. The discoverer was merely the first one to be convinced by the new opinion on the basis of its evidence, its truth. As I said, the intellectual first empties himself so as to make room for the reception and manifestation of the new truth. This makes sense of the intellectual's revolt against public opinion.

At this point we can formulate with greater precision the nature of the mammoth attempt afoot today to quash the intellectual's collaboration in human affairs: in a strict sense, the debate today turns on whether truth is manifest in the individual, in one person, or in collective life, in a people. However, since those who talk most about social groups never seem to have the slightest notion about what the word means, or the problems involved, we have no choice but to dedicate part of these lectures to an exact and unambiguous definition of a whole series of concepts, such as collectivity, society, people, nation, internation, ultranation, state, right, law, custom, use, disuse, abuse, and so forth. As you can see, even though this is only one of the facets or aspects of our course, it will occupy a considerable part of our time.

Here is the second general observation: it does not suffice for an opinion to be evident, and hence true, for it to win acceptance. Mankind is not spontaneously open, predis-

posed, or receptive to evidence. Instead this predisposition
is what an intellectual struggles to cultivate in himself: it is
his technique and his craft. How, then, does he inject the
giant monolith of public opinion with his own opinions?
How does he conqueor it? It is impossible for the intellectual to withstand the sheer force of passions, appetites, special interests, and inertia that make up public opinion.
Intellect has no strength at all; it is by nature un-dynamic.
Ideas are pure transparency—incorporeal, luminous ghosts.
What chance have they against the tremendous force of social
impulses? (The first thinkers may be pardoned for their
aggressive and irritating tone, for striking a boxer's stance;
they had as yet no experience of their peculiar innovative
abilities.) But in a short while the spirit, intelligence, realized that, since the quid of its mission was to counter enormous, incoercible forces, instead of fighting them toe to toe,
on the contrary it should work by attraction, charm, and
seduction. Because intelligence was without strength, it must
then exercise its powers of attraction. And, in fact, throughout history, intelligence has been a sort of snake-charmer,
taming the snakes and dragons of impulsiveness. In this it
is only imitating God: the *theós*, Aristotle's god, is the supreme
being and the prime mover of the universe. But it doesn't
move the world with the push of a finger or the exertions of
a day-laborer. The prime mover is the unmoved mover of
the world. He moves it by attracting it to his perfection,
fascinating it with his splendor; to explain this difficult idea
Aristotle uses one of the most famous and acute metaphors
in the history of thought, when he says that God moves the
world "as the beloved moves the lover." And the beloved
moves the lover by transporting him—by enchanting, fascinating, and seducing him. Now then, sketched in substance and form, this is why we have intellectuals; their
mission on earth is to oppose and to seduce.

3

Uniforms and authenticity. The *genus dicendi* of
the major philosophers. Intention and ambiguity. My style. Perform an activity and will to do
so. The elements of the human task. Simultane-
ous and successive situations. Propositional function. Conceptual schema. Philosophy, something
men do. Present situation of intelligence.
Husserl. Crisis of principles in the sciences.
Iberian man's irresponsible speech habits. Final
court of appeal. Annihilation of rights.

IN THE FIRST TWO LECTURES I made an effort to show as
starkly as possible how everywhere in the world today intellectuals are seen as expendable. If I feel this is so for the
intellectual *in genere* and without exception, you can imagine how convinced I must be of the questionableness of my
own position, since I am more conscious than anyone of my
very real limitations. Since the latter were never a secret to
me, I accepted them as a matter of course and fitted my life
into an extremely questionable mold; I expected to be questionable and, hence, questioned; I never tried to protect
myself by hiding my head in the diving helmet of a weighty
ministry, or to disguise myself as the figurehead of a traditional or a clearly defined institutional life. In these lectures
we shall see precisely how any form of life that is already
there, constituted, defined, crystalized, and offering itself
as a pre-established mold into which we pour the flowing

liquid of our life, is always and in essence an inauthentic form of life. Which does not mean that this inauthenticity is without a necessary, inevitable, and beneficial aspect. Perhaps no one suspects this now (it will be obvious by mid-course), but what I have just said contains the entire problem of the "social"—what society and collective life are—about which so much has been said with so little real knowledge. Professions, offices, ministries, all are inauthentic life-forms. So, in equal measure, are the official, consecrated stereotypes of the novelist, the engineer, the philosopher, and all the other professions that tradition and practice have turned into something like carnival masks—from which people expect certain behavior and which are recognized by typical attributes the way we recognize the allegory of Justice by her scales—carnival masks with which people feel comfortable because they always know what to expect. Equivalent to a soldier's uniform, which helps us recognize him at a distance, there is the physical and mental uniform of the poet or the philosopher. It is impossible to convince people that these carnival masks were always false; it is useless to point out that neither Hannibal, nor Caesar, nor Napoleon wore a "uniform." Useless to say that Plato dressed like an elegant Athenian, since he belonged to their highest aristocracy, or that Leibniz dressed like a marquis at Versailles, that even Emmanuel Kant, who was of modest origins, dressed like a dandy even though he never left Königsberg—the little, provincial capital where he was born. And quite useless to remind them that Parmenides, founder of metaphysics, wrote one poem only; that Plato wrote only pleasant dialogues of great poetry—except, of course, for his complicated dialogue *Parmenides*, which is anyway of uncertain authorship—that Aristotle, ah, Aristotle!, published only one book, his *Nicomachean Ethics*, that Platonic-style dialogue of which only fragments survive, but which allows us to see how marvelous it was; and that it was, moreover, his only work that influenced his contemporaries. It is useless to recall that Descartes founded no less than the modern era, and especially modern philosophy, with an essay whose style or *genus dicendi* imitates the writings of Montaigne—his famous *Discourse on Method* (in which it seems not a word is said of philosophy and only slightly more about method, but instead is just what one would expect, in French and in an autobiography, which was every bit as much a scandal then for the professors at the Sorbonne as my "literary" writings are in Lisbon)—or that at the end of his life he wanted to pen the first complete exposition of his system in a dialogue having the form of a mundane conversation between Eudoxio, Polyandre, and Episthemon. This was his *Recherche de la Vérité par la lumière naturelle*, which, had he finished it, would have been one of the most marvellous books in all philosophy. Similarly, Leibniz scarcely wrote anything other than pleasant dialogues—that is, his famous *Theodicea* and his *New Essays on Human Understanding*, and so forth. We could go on forever in this vein because it is rich and wide and much more important than certain philosophers suppose, who talk philosophy "by ear" the way some people play the guitar. For my part, if I once get angry, which is unlikely—because, as we shall see, there are weighty and essential reasons why philosophers should never get angry—I shall grasp some pseudo-intellectual by the lapels and demand his clearest ideas on the style of Aristotle's *Metaphysics*, his *Physics*, his *On the Soul*, and his *Organon*. Because this will be a question about which the aforesaid pseudo-intellectual quite naturally knows nothing. Anyway, we have no time for such skirmishes. I only meant that people seem to expect philosophers to be poorly dressed, to have dandruff on their shoulders, and to speak or write in textbook-*Handbuch*-vade mecum-style; anything else frustrates their stereotyped expectations. This explains the sharpness with which I just spoke—but, considering the times, I hope it won't shock you too much.*

People, and often those who feel most expert, need carnival masks, uniforms, wrappings. Without disguises they feel lost, and this irritates them. They are incapable of seeing clearly and unblinkingly, without preconceptions, what reality sets before them, which, in truth, always turns out to be singular and concrete, always new and unforeseen: the very opposite of a ready-made mask, a wrapping, a consecrated uniform. Thus the person who intends to follow a pattern usually ends up behind a mask or a uniform. This is just what I decided not to do, because I didn't want to be any of those well-known and illustrious "pre-things." I only wanted to be, to work at being . . . ; we'll soon see with what degree of success. My limitations aside, how could I not help seeming the most questionable and ambiguous being imaginable? *I believe only in ambiguity*, because reality itself is that way; and anything that is a simplification and that means to be unequivocal is an adulteration and a falsification of reality, a commonplace notion, a floundering about, a pose. This is why if anyone ever has sufficient curiosity and surplus interest to take up what I do and what I am, I shall be first surprised and shall then thank them with quite real and amazed sincerity. But I simply will not be what others want me to be—a carnival mask, a uniform, a wrapping! And just as I only esteem those men or women from whom I never know what to expect, so I like others not to

---

*Because it has to be said that nothing new, important, or creative has ever been introduced into philosophy in a book or discourse in the textbook-*Handbuch*-vade mecum-style, or in a soporific lesson addressed to college students. But the university is not a college; it is not even solely for students. The whole nation should participate in university intellectual life, and this means that gifted workers should also take part. When a university is only its students and nothing of national importance, and in this sense nothing popular happens there, it is a sign that the university has decayed to the extent that by a process of involution it has become a species of college for pre-schoolers. But to achieve this participation we must give up the Manual-*Handbuch*-vade mecum-style—for which I have the lowest regard—in our general courses. [Ortega. Insertion by Ed.]

know what to expect from me, to wonder if I am a philosopher or a poet or if, perhaps, I am neither but a rare duck-billed platypus—an apposite theme, that one. By behaving in this imprecise and unclassifiable way, I imagine I pay others the most profoundly respectful, the most fruitful, the greatest homage I can.

But all this is said primarily to thank you for the unexpected interest my lectures have awakened in Lisbon, and the generous number of you who attend—in fact, since the large public has become a too-large public, the director of the Faculty has had to move us out of his professional domain. So that this Chair of Philosophy has become a nomad, wandering over the earth—over the *Geo*—and has now pitched its Bedouin tent in the Geographical Society. But for that very reason I must expressly ask you to bear in mind that the table before me continues to be *formally* the Chair of Philosophy of the Humanities Faculty of Lisbon University—even though its shape and material are somewhat changed. I want all those listening to keep this in mind, first of all, because it is the simple truth, since the accident of our needing more space does not alter the substance of my words; and second, because my way of "holding" a Chair is "exquisite" as you have seen, and my style of address *ex cathedra* is already well-known to you—it has not changed appreciably in thirty-four years (I began shortly after I turned twenty) as far as my general courses are concerned, although my seminars and advanced teaching are another matter. This style of address requires, as an essential ingredient, that it emanate or proceed from a Chair, in the most traditional and ordinary sense, that is, it needs constantly to rest against it.

I said in the last lecture that the least one can say of philosophy is that it is something man does.* It is one of the

* In the original text that has survived the 'previous' statement referred to here is absent. It is probably to be found in the missing pages, which I mentioned earlier. [Ed.]

countless tasks *[haceres]* man has. "*Haceres*"—the plural of
"*hacer*" [to do, to make]—is not a usual Spanish word but a
neologism. Perhaps you can say something similar in Portuguese: "*os faceres.*" I would be hard put to renounce this
new word since it contains a concept I shall use often and
the meaning of which, therefore, I will forthwith explain.

Some days ago I was wandering in the square called das
Amoreiras, which is one of the prettiest in Lisbon and
deserves to be better known. Off to one side is a *cantiño* [a
corner] called Alto de San Francisco, which is marvellous
and I recommend it to the painters of the new style. I call
it Picasso Square. Well, as I drifted about that quiet, hidden
place I was going over this lecture. A friend passed and
asked me: "What are you doing here?" And I answered:
"Strolling and thinking a bit." Apparently I was doing two
things. It occurred to me that our brief exchange could be
an example for today's lecture.

Strolling is moving one's legs so as to advance slowly over
solid ground—a kind of walking. It is an act our muscles
perform without our "I" intervening; it is organic activity.
Man houses an enormous number of organic activities the
body performs on its own: digestion, circulation of fluids,
breathing, and so forth. These are all physiological, somatic,
or bodily mechanisms that function automatically. Not only
do they function independently of our will; the will cannot
effect some of them even if it wants to—as with digestion
or the circulation of the blood. In others—walking, for
example—our will can intervene but only to begin, continue, or stop their functioning and their manner, as with
walking faster or slower. But our will does not intervene in
the activity itself. Therefore, in a sense, "I" don't do them.
Doing something, then, is not a simple activity. Then why
did I answer the friend who asked what I was "doing" by
saying "strolling"? If I recall what I meant, if I explicate the
meaning I gave "doing," I arrive at the following: my body

performed the activity "walking," but I had wanted it so—
and this was why I felt I was "doing" it. Doing, then, has
two factors or ingredients:

1. The actual performance of an activity of which we are
capable.

2. The will to perform it or to want it.

I might have been walking around that square in my sleep.
The performance would have been the same, but I wouldn't
have willed it—then I wouldn't have been "doing" it. There
is thus one wandering, walking, or strolling that is a doing,
and another that is a plain and simple organic activity—
what is called sleepwalking, or somnambulism.

The same is true of the other thing I was doing: thinking.
It doesn't matter whether we are fantasizing or imagining
or thinking *sensu stricto*, that is, in a formal sense. In our
mind, chains of images appear; the production of these is a
mental activity called imagination, fantasy, or memory,
depending on whether the images belong to a particular past
or not. I "find" images there just as I find myself surrounded by a world, with visible shapes, audible sounds—
without having invented them. I don't invent my images or
memories. Imagination and memory are mental mechanisms that function by themselves. What can and often does
happen is that we decide to imagine or decide to remember,
that is, deliberately and voluntarily set off or start up these
mechanisms; a novelist, for instance, imagines the plot of a
novel, or a man begins to write his memoirs. Both set off—
will—the activity of imagining and remembering, but neither intervenes in the activity itself, nor can he do so. Once
it is provoked, set in motion, the activity functions automatically.

An image that suddenly comes to me does not appear as
though I were its source. This is why our expression "I
imagine" is strictly speaking incorrect. Because the active
verb not only signifies the activity—imagining, in this case—

it also means or signifies that this activity proceeds from the grammatical subject. This is why verbs have personal conjugations, that is, change their lexical form according to their grammatical subject; and this is why there is a first, second, and third person, singular and plural, and why even in the plural some languages distinguish between an exclusive and an inclusive plural; in Greek there is a dual person, which requires that two and no more effect the action; and the Melanesian languages, Kivai, for example, even have a triple person, that is, a tri-agent form; and in other languages the verb form changes according to the agent's sex. The extreme case is the language of primitive peoples, such as the Polynesians, where an activity such as eating or walking is expressed by verbs with different roots according to whether the agent is the king or one of his subjects. This is the supreme measure of the extent to which an active verb signals its origin or source in the subject of the activity.

For this reason I call the expression "I imagine" incorrect, since it does not denote a pure and authentic phenomenon. "Phenomenon": this is a silly word we philosophers have to struggle with since we inherited it from one of our most brilliant teachers, most brilliant but also most inexcusably pedantic, from Kant, in a word—although Wolf and Leibniz, writing in Latin, had already used it. The word "phenomenon" means quite simply all that we have, or what appears to us when we take it just as it appears to us, without adding anything or taking anything away. In this case what we have or what appears to us is our act of imagining, and if we pay attention to what is there, we realize it is not that I imagine but rather that I find the images there, and thus instead of my producing or calling up the images, *something else* does.

The same happens with seeing, hearing, and the other senses. They are activities in which I don't intervene; I can only stop them by closing my eyes, covering my ears—or help them along by looking hard for something or by sharpening my hearing. Here our language clearly distinguishes between the mere activity and doing it voluntarily—since it speaks of mere looking and of seeing, or of mere listening and of hearing. Indeed, the identical thing happens with thinking in the most formal sense—which consists of a series of automatic operations such as discriminating, identifying, comparing, inferring, and so forth. Thinking sometimes takes place spontaneously, at other times it is set in motion by my "I"—when we decide to think. But we still do not intervene in the activity itself. Thinking is a mental mechanism and not more than that, albeit one that is more or less at our disposal like the razor we shave with or the elevator in our building. But the surprising thing is—and I referred to it at the start of these lectures as a theme of more general philosophical interest than you would suppose—even the thought that engenders the most formal concepts imaginable sometimes functions so suddenly and unexpectedly that its products, instead of seeming to be our creation, give the impression of something we stumble upon like a stone in our path. This is why some of the most complicated mathematical problems have been solved in sleep, even though their discoverer had been vainly trying to resolve them for years. The best and most famous example is Poincaré's solution of the Fuchsian functions, which he describes in detail. Just as there is sleepwalking, there is also sleep*thinking*.

Thus it is our willing or wanting it that makes an activity a human task *[hacer]* However, our willing always has an object, and beyond that we want it for some reason and to some purpose. The gentleman listening there shifted in his chair because he was uncomfortable, and to find a more comfortable position. The *why* of our wanting we term the motive, [what] motivates our want. The *what for* of our activity we call its goal or purpose. And I appeal to the extreme humility and triviality of the example of shifting in one's chair to suggest that *why* the gentleman moves—his *motive*—is what we call a necessity or human need, and the *what for* of it, the new, more comfortable position—his purpose—is, no less, no more, than what we call an ideal, a term heavy with cant and romanticism. The grand illustrious ideals that guide a man's entire life or a people's or all humanities' are no more ideals than this very unillustrious desire to be more comfortable that exercised our gentleman on his hard chair.

Therefore, the decisive factor in human tasks is that we will them. They are voluntary acts, willed by man, and for this reason he is evidently their generator, their cause, and the one responsible for them. But in this willing we also find—as a primary element—a motive, *a tèrgo*, that moves or mobilizes, that lies behind it and moves it along. But this motive always arises from a *situation*. In truth, *why* we do something is always to be sought in our situation, to which we react by willing a better one, and for the purpose of obtaining another one we prefer; this is why we decide to perform an activity, carry out an action. *A human task is unintelligible until we discover or envision the situation in which it arose.*

Who knows? Perhaps the *why* and the *what for* of human tasks may hold the key to what is very likely the most fundamental problem of all, so fundamental that not only has philosophy not explained it, it has not even managed to pose the problem—the problem of intelligibility itself, in other words, how we explain or at least begin to elucidate, the absolutely mysterious fact that the universe contains what we call meaning, *nous* (the intelligible as such, what occasions our understanding or not understanding), and, therefore, what we are able to think—for what we understand is the meaning of a sentence, and what we don't understand is its meaninglessness. This is the weighty question that Cicero, following the Stoics, called *lumen naturale*, an idea he passed on to Saint Augustine and the Neoplatonists. But what neither the Stoics nor, of course, Cicero, nor even Saint Augustine or the Neoplatonists bothered to explain was its consistency, except for Saint Augustine saying that it comes to us from God; but here he was only following that quite respectable but much too comfortable custom of burdening God with all the incomprehensible things that befall man. But let us leave this thorny problem for the present.

In each moment man is in a specific general situation that can be subdivided into lesser parts, even the smallest and most humble of which also deserves to be thought of as a situation. No matter how minute and insignificant it seems, it is still a situation or position inasmuch as this is what the word "situation" means. Situation comes from *situs*, the participle of *sino*, to place or leave something. You see how much more than you supposed was contained in the trivial example of the man uncomfortable in his seat.

In my lectures, ladies and gentlemen—and allow me to point this out so that, inasmuch as you have made this generous effort to attend, what I have to say will be of use and you may make the most of it—in my lectures, as you see, alertness is all, because quite often an example I introduce—apparently unimportant and casually chosen, seemingly in jest—turns out to be, in spite of the humor, quite heavy with meaning. And this is what chuckleheaded intellectuals have in mind when they speak of the literariness of my lectures. It would be a sorry pass if my lectures weren't literary at all! I wonder what view of literature these chuckleheads have!

Thus, the listener who is uncomfortable in his seat is in a situation, albeit an extremely simple, bodily one which, for that very reason, is a minute component of a larger situation: the one you are all in now, here in this room listening to a philosophy, or perhaps a literary, lecture—it isn't clear which. You are all, then, in a very ambiguous situation. But the latter, in turn, for those of you who are citizens here (being Portuguese in the year 1944 A.D.), is located in an even larger and more substantial situation, which would be the situation Portugal is in today. Yet this is also part of a world situation. And since the present general world situation was preceded by countless others, we can see that universal history is the entire situation of mankind, which encompasses all the other situations and makes up the entire, concrete reality that has been the destiny of man in its complete historical unfolding down to the present. The list of the situations that man has been in is extremely long. Calculations based on geological studies, especially those having to do with glacial periods, allow us to say, for the first time with any certainty, that mankind has been on earth a million years. Make no mistake; that's time enough to allow for a multitude of varied situations! Still, no matter how varied these have been, they have enough characteristics in common for us to say they are all human life situations. If we isolate their identical, shared, permanent characteristics, which are the substrate of countless, extremely diverse situations, we arrive at what can properly be called "human life," which, therefore, is itself a "situation," *the* situation— the essential one—which *consists in* being human. This is why W. Macneile Dixon, the English writer, gave his book the elegant title, *The Human Situation.* A pity the most interesting thing about his book is its title!

This brief analysis of *tasks* permits us to give two clear formulations of the question: first, through the explicit list of its moments or ingredients that I read before.

The second formulation is symbolic and consists in a rigorous formula in the strict mathematical sense of the word. In fact, it is like an algebraic formula or a physical law; what is more, it is the purest of logical expressions, or what new or mathematical logic terms a "judgment function" or "propositional function"—in which there are certain variables and certain constants. This is no time to explain the meaning of propositional function or formal expression. We shall go into this, in depth, later on because it is the universal key or instrument with which to think efficiently about any problem, whether it be scientific or practical. But I should like to leave this marvellous instrument with you—about which not nearly enough has been said, not even by its inventor—so as to repay you for your attention. Reduced to its bare essentials the formula is designed to give symbolic expression—in words and signs—to the structure of human tasks, to what they are or, in the terminology explained in the last lecture, to their generic consistency. While the possible human tasks are infinite in number and are all more or less different, they have certain constituent elements in common that permit us to call them all, no matter how varied, by the same name: "task." So that in every human task there are some constants and some variable elements, the latter different in each case.

The constants of our formula are in performing an activity—the task's *why* and its *what for*. Since these are constants, in the formula they can be called by their proper names; on the other hand, the variable elements, which are always distinct, must be represented by empty signs that indicate the gaps in the formula that we are to fill, in each case, with the corresponding specifics. Thus, if we apply this formla to the simple, concrete case of the listener shifting in his chair, we fill the gap represented by A (the concrete Activity carried out) with "to shift in a chair"; in the gap designated M (Motive) we put "uncomfortable physical position"; and in the space P (Purpose) we put "to be more comfortable." An algebraic formula, a propositional function or, as I prefer to put it, more simply—which is what really matters in philosophy (as distinct from mathematics and logic, as we shall see)—a *conceptual schema*, consists of constants and gaps: *leere stelle*, empty spaces, as German mathematicians say. If there is a human task we need to clarify, we have only to use this formula, taking from the task whatever corresponds to the gaps in the formula. As you can see, this is all as simple as "Good Morning"; just as simple and just as boring. Unfortunately, we have no choice but to have our several intellectual instruments clean and well sharpened. The inevitable moment for the exposition of our "task-formula" is at hand because what I am about to say, which formally marks the positive and dogmatic beginning of our course, requires such a formula in order to establish the relationship between tasks and what I have called "situation."

Now we can return to where we said that the least one can say about philosophy is that it is something man does. Because now, to have a clear idea of the task philosophy is, we know we must backtrack to the situation that elicited it, since even philosophy is merely a specific reaction to a specific situation. When changes in the situation are minimal, philosophic thought needs to change very little and so drags sleepily along in its usual guise, so that as far as the general public is concerned philosophy is then about as difficult to board as a slowly moving streetcar.

But when a fundamental change takes place in the situation—understand by this a *radical* change, one calling for new roots and, hence, a prior *uprootedness*—philosophy has no alternative but to be just as radical in its reaction and to revise its perennial problems in a *radical* way, to renew the whole repertoire of its basic concepts, including, perhaps, the most basic ones of all, and as a secondary, inevitable consequence, its vocabulary, its mode of discourse and presentation.

The truth is that we are at present in the midst of just such a radical change. A philosophy that *is* current—in contrast to the philosophies that *were* current—must take its departure from the present situation of the intellect; and herewith we arrive, somewhat out of practice and having taken on too much, at the point I had hoped to reach in my first lecture.

What change has overtaken the situation of the intellect, of reason? Philosophy was born—as will be seen in detail at a future date—as the discovery of the intellect, of reason. It has been, therefore, inevitably linked to the fate of intellectual reason. Any change they have undergone has affected it profoundly. We must then ask what change has come about, what change we are involved in now.

Fortunately, on this point I can be brief, self-assured, and dogmatic. I need only read the following paragraph by Edmund Husserl, that is, by the philosopher who in this century has undoubtedly had the greatest influence on philosophical studies. The following paragraph is from the last book he published, *Formal and Transcendental Logic*, 1929:

"The present condition of European sciences necessitates radical investigations of sense. At bottom these sciences have lost their great belief in themselves, in their absolute significance. The modern man of today, unlike the 'modern' man of the Enlightenment, does not behold in science the self-Objectivation of human reason or the universal activity mankind has devised for itself in order to make possible a truly satisfying life, an individual and social life of practical reason. The belief that science leads to wisdom—to an actually rational self-cognition and cognition of the world and God, and, by means of such cognition, to a life somehow to be shaped closer to perfection, a life truly worth living, a life of "happiness," contentment, well-being, or the like—this great belief, once the substitute for religious belief, has (at least in wide circles) lost its force. Thus men live entirely in a world that has become unintelligible, in which they ask in vain for the wherefore, the sense, which was once so certain and accepted by the understanding, as well as by the will. . . ."

But this interprets the paragraph I read from Husserl in a general way and, so to say, as observed from without.* Clearly there is more to what he says, behind what he says, and to which his words allude, because Husserl was a fortunate philosopher in the sense that he could address an audience of scientific-minded men who were knowledgeable about the science of the day, which is the only real science.

And, in fact, notice that Husserl says "these sciences have lost their great belief in themselves." It is not the case, then, that the man in the street questions science, nor simply that the social situation of the intellectual has changed—I spoke about the latter for numerous, important reasons, among them the need to contrast the situation of the intellectual with the situation of the intellect, so that their difference would be clear. It is not even the case here that the scientist is wavering in his belief in science, not at all—but *that science itself has lost confidence in itself.* And since science cannot abide vagueness and generalities, this lack of confidence can only have a rigorous and terribly precise configuration, which is to say, science's lack of confidence in itself must be a scientific truth.

This is the question; *it is nothing less than this.* There are three sciences that together make up the Acropolis, the fortress of the intelligence or reason, three that were one with it: physics, mathematics, and logic. They were the dense, solid base on which humankind rested, especially for the last few centuries. The solidity of this ample base provided the nutrient for the faith in reason that has been the invisible support on which man has based his life for the last twenty-five hundred years—because Christianity, religious faith since the days of Saint Anselm, or since the eleventh century, has been obliged to depend on reason, on intelligence, a need expressed programmatically in the phrase *Fides*

---

*The text containing Ortega's interpretation is from his untranslated "Notes on Thinking." [Ed.]

querens intellectus (Let faith seek out intellect). If these sciences—physics, mathematics, logic—ever felt the slightest uncertainty, the whole world of reason would tremble and be at risk. Yet the fact is that for the last thirty years the extraordinary development of science has been accompanied by an increasing uneasiness. The physicist, the mathematician, and the logician have discovered, for the first time in the history of science, that bottomless, problematic abysses have suddenly opened in the fundamental principles of their theories. And these principles were the only solid basis for their intellectual operations. Yet it was precisely here, in what seemed most sound, and not in some backwater of their theoretical organisms, that the abysses appeared.

If there is anything fundamental about physics it is the concept of matter and the principle of causality; but matter had turned to smoke in the physicist's hands, and *there was no longer such a thing as matter*. The principle of causality, was already weakened when the new physics started to deal primarily in statistical rather than constitutive laws—we'll explain the difference another day— or (and, provisionally, it amounts to the same thing) ever since the truth of knowledge in physics was downgraded from truth pure and simple to probable truth, to mere probability. Speaking *grosso modo*, we can express this by saying that physics no longer tries to tell us that things are this way or the other, but only that they *probably* are this way or that, and this downgrading of the truth of physics received its final turn with the uncertainty principle that accompanied the discovery of those luminous "quanta." Since there is no longer any matter, there is no causality, which is to say that both principles are called into question. The situation in physics is such that for the last fifteen years the specialized journals have been publishing articles in which physicists ask each other what their formulae refer to, if any reality corresponds to what they speak of, or if their formulae are merely useful inventions and, consequently—notice the extreme gravity of this, ladies and gentlemen—they wondered if they could still call physics *knowledge*. I don't expect you to gather the full import of this; there is no need to do so now. It will soon be perfectly clear. Now you only need to notice one momentous fact—unthinkable fifty years ago—which is what the physicists (mind you, the physicists, not the philosophers) think about physics. Here it is: they confess they aren't quite sure what they are doing when they do physics.

This is what nowadays is called "the crisis of the foundations" of the sciences. Because a similar thing is happening in mathematics and, to an even greater degree, in logic. But logic is the science of the *lògos*, of reason—the very essence of reason. Until a short while ago logic continued to be more or less what its first codifier, Aristotle, had made it—and Aristotle's logic was only the outline of a few small areas of logic. Thus, strictly speaking, logic was only an admirable project, a fairly precise program, but no more than a program and not its accomplishment. However, recently when a profound attempt was made *to construct logic*, and to have it *exist* in fact and not just in the illusion of a program, this proved to be impossible; *among other things* its most important principle—the law of the excluded middle—proved to be false. Now one reads something even more extraordinary: the brilliant mathematical logician—the brilliant Dutch mathematician, Brouwer—whose influence in both sciences has been vast, if not the most pervasive, has spoken disdainfully of logic as *soi-disant* logic.

Soi-disant logic! Do you realize the enormity of this? It means, quite simply, that logic is illogical, that, therefore, there is no logic. All this I call the earthquake in reason—and the image is no exaggeration.

(There may be, ladies and gentlemen—and remember that I refer to imaginary people and have no reason for thinking that anyone has reacted in this way, although it is not all that unlikely given the age we live in and the conditions of Iberian Man—there may be those who when they hear this will say with their easy, customary petulance that they couldn't care less about this. These are people who try to make life easy for themselves, and *the easiest thing of all is to say very dogmatic things*, irresponsible, gratuitous things. But life is not easy; what is easy is to speak that way: to say they couldn't care less about something or other; but I doubt whether this apparent not caring is really sincere. In the present instance at least one thing is certain: the very minimum requirement or condition for not caring that intelligence has reached a stage where logic has ceased to exist or, equally, where logic has been called into question would be that one at least understand what this means and its consequences. In truth these imaginary people have not the slightest idea what this means, and so they *say* they couldn't care less—because that's easy enough—but they don't mean it because that would be too hard for them. Some day we shall have to discuss fully this habit of irresponsible speech that is one of the most serious vices of Iberian Man, on both sides of our gentle frontier, where part of my heritage lies—in Olivenza, a town that was always unsure if it belonged to Portugal or to Spain, so that, uncertain about many things, I sometimes awake saying: Could I be Portuguese? I repeat, we shall have to speak of this irresponsible manner of speaking, characteristic of Iberian Man and related to his native insolence and his accustomed petulance, because this vice undermines any serious attempt at communal life, it destroys all possible cooperation and hence any collective life to a creative, constructive purpose —no matter what its political cast or how different the participants are. Notice that by "irresponsible manner of speaking" I don't just mean saying things without rhyme or reason, without objective basis and just to hear the sound of their own voice; no, the worst thing about this brand of irresponsibility is that the speaker has not even managed to match what he says to what he really thinks and feels. So on the one hand speaking this way fails to match the truth of the things spoken of, and, on the other, it fails to coincide with the essence of the speaker, it is a kind of "free" speech, floating like milkweed, with no paternity at all. So that—let me offer this advice—perhaps not always, certainly not, but often we would be naive and confused if we assumed that Iberian Man thought or felt a certain way because of what he said. If Iberian Man so often fails to agree with anything or anyone, it isn't because of what is flatteringly called his "individualism," but simply because the typical Iberian Man, I have no other in mind, begins by not even agreeing with himself, by lacking solidarity with himself. Since I am well along in years and our Iberia is the thing I have thought most about, I know Iberian Man, and he can't deceive me or confound me. I know all his hidden sides, all his invisible, inner mechanisms, and one day—but not here—in some essay I will expose those insides to public scrutiny and subject them to a detailed anatomical study so everyone can see them. Because in times as tremendously hard as these, it is so difficult to do anything with such a man that we must undertake the unflagging reform of his very innards.)

Soi-disant logic! Formerly logic was the benchmark, the final appeals court before which all other discourse, thinking, and, therefore, all reality had to appear and be judged either authentic or merely *soi-disant*, fictitious, false, would-be. But now the benchmark itself has turned *soi-disant*, would-be, that is, something inauthentic and basically questionable. The final appeals court itself has become problematic; the highest judge is now the accused criminal.

Those who are younger will see, in future years, the extent to which it is *not* a matter of no concern to have to live together without any final appeals court. Because the threat that logic will go up in smoke and be just another human utopia, another vain illusion that has lasted twenty-five hundred years—logic was discovered about 480 B.C.—means, quite simply, that the very notion of truth is on the wane; and thus, in a real sense, if this threat is a fact and no remedy is found, there will cease to be true or false things, nothing will have its own, clear-cut being, and the light that truth represents in the primordial darkness of our lives will be extinguished and darkness will reign.

But the earthquake has occurred not only in scientific or theoretical reason, but also in practical reason, and at the same time. I shall skip morality, which, as the rational law of conduct, went up in smoke some forty years ago, leaving the weight of custom as the sole regulator of human behavior. Instead, in recent times we have witnessed an unimaginable spectacle that will surely have disturbed anyone who understands it. I refer to the complete disappearance of law. But since this is rough terrain, and since I want no misunderstandings and wrong interpretations, I have written out several pages that you will have to listen to me read.

Law, ladies and gentlemen, together with truth—but even more than truth, because it is historically much, much older—seemed to be always the essential ingredient in human society. It took tens of thousands of years to discover, institute, and consolidate it. The specific contents—that is, laws in the plural, individual laws—varied from nation to nation or changed, evolved with imperceptible or age-long slowness within each nation, but their common ground, the faith that there *was law*, which by definition is the final appeals court to which men in disagreement turn (we shall explain to what extent *laws are in essence a recourse*), the faith that there was law, has never been absent. Yet we have been so original as to lose this faith as well. For this is not a question of replacing a worn-out set of laws with new and vigorous ones; this happened before, although it was always a more serious undertaking than anyone supposed, and they underestimated it accordingly because nothing is so little known as the consistency of law. This ignorance includes everyone from politicians who, naturally, because they are politicians usually don't know anything anyway—we shall also examine in depth what it means to be a politician, regardless of party or program—this ignorance, as I said, includes politicians, jurists, and even philosophers of law. This is one of the most disgraceful things about our contemporary era!

Today, then, we are not faced with another substitution of new for old laws (supposing, that is, "new laws" are not oddities like "square circles"—we'll see about that). For the first time in the history of Europe what has happened is that the system of laws, of institutions is seen to be exhausted, without there having appeared on the horizon any new laws or institutions to replace them. They are nowhere, not even in the airy form of pure theoretical ideas in the minds of a few thinkers. So that those who today trample all laws—without a single one remaining intact on earth—have no notion, no moderately clear idea of what laws to put in their place. I call this, without too much exaggeration, the annihilation of law. And it would be a delusion to object that in some countries certain domestic laws have not been broken. If this hasn't happened yet it is not because they are laws but because in those countries the occasion for their breaking has not arisen, which does not mean—far from it—that the occasion will not arise sooner or later. Time, that *galant'uomo*, according to Cardinal Mazarin, will tell.

The most obvious example of this universal destruction of law is the supression of the minimal right of neutrality. *Let me be perfectly clear:* I am not discussing or arguing whether this or that country should be neutral at a certain time in a particular war. That would be to talk and argue politics, a thing I not only cannot do here but would not even if I could, because it is neither my calling nor my duty, and especially since I have such a low opinion of politics, both bad and good politics—if the latter exists—of all politics. This will be clear in an absolute sense when we speak seriously of what society is, and the state, and public power, and rights, and law, when we actively and unflinchingly face the question of why such a thing as politics should exist at all; it seems unlikely, yet no one has yet made this a substantive issue, that is, not good politics as opposed to bad, or vice versa, but strictly and without adornment, the plain question of what politics is.

I only refer to the abrogation of the law of neutrality as a small example that mirrors the disappearance of all law—of the consciousness of law and of the faith in law—in exactly the same spirit, and for just the same reason that I spoke of the concept of matter going up in smoke, along with the principle of causality in physics and the law of the excluded middle in mathematical logic, in short, as different examples of the present dramatic situation that has overtaken theoretical reason.

But even though I am no one and have never tried to be more than I am, it is a fact that what I say is heard in distant places, and this means that beyond Iberia what I have just said and what follows has to be perfectly clear, so that I disown any reproduction, extract, or interpretation that does not consist in exactly the words I read.

The supression of the right to neutrality that begins with the interdiction of free trade on the part of the neutral country and leads to interference with its postal service and the violation of the secrecy of correspondence, and ends with a forced alliance with one of the belligerents, is a clear sign of the complete destruction in the world of any consciousness of law. Because with the abrogation of this particular right — neutrality with all its attributes—nothing is put in its place and the emptiness can only be filled by the decisions of the powerful nations. Now then, I want to make it perfectly clear that in saying this I do not mean that the conduct lead-

ing to this interdiction is necessarily, and in all cases, a for-
bidden and unforgivable mode of conduct. I am prepared to
follow to its foreseeable conclusion the specific duty of the
intellectual, which, as I said the other day, obliges him to
consider that anything is possible in principle and that the
strangest events can make sense. So that in this regard there
might be substantive major pressures heretofore unknown
that call for the interdiction of the law of neutrality, pressures perhaps due, not to current circumstances—the problems of which are of a consistency and enormity unknown
until now—but to the direction or *drift* of the last two centuries, which with a continual and overwhelming force is
now destroying all rights, and which caused Royer-Collard
to remark as long ago as 1830 that he everywhere saw "events
that were force" but nowhere "things that were law." What
seems to me significant is that the act whereby in interdict-
ing one law all laws are symbolically interdicted, could come
about in two opposite ways: either those responsible, forced
to this extreme—let us suppose—by circumstances, behave
thus with the clear and painful consciousness of the unlimited gravity that their action implies, and of the possibility
of unleashing decades and decades of *bellum omnium contra
omnes,* as in the most disastrous stages of human history; or
else they behave thus with a *gaîté de coeur,* as the French say,
gaily and with total innocence of the implications; in a word,
senselessly. I would like to believe the former is now the
case but I am not sure this is so. And the main reason for
my unwelcome suspicion is my observation, not so much of
what politicians do, as of the way the intellectuals of the
leading nations deal with the enormous problems of the present, and I include the war years and the immediate prewar
years. I am an intellectual belonging to a minor nation, and
as an individual I am not so much, yet I am, however modest, good at my job, and so without any undue pretension

on my part I say to the world's intellectuals from this Lusitanian corner, and out of my own insignificance (and I say this as to colleagues in a guild whose statutes allow neither vagueness nor evasions), that the serious and taciturn intellectuals of the minor Latin nations who accepted the teachings of the great nations with enthusiasm and a justified humility—my life has been an extreme example of this and no one can accuse me of lacking reverence, of indocility, or of being remiss in wanting to learn—we intellectuals of the minor Latin nations notice with shame and sorrow the superficiality, the theoretical weakness, the complete lack of acuity and depth with which the great intellectuals of the major nations have dealt in recent years with contemporary problems in their books and journals. And if we notice their ignorance as intellectuals no one should be surprised if we are somewhat frightened of a possible future ignorance on the part of politicians. I am prepared to try to demonstrate this, wherever I am invited to do so, only provided I am given enough time to say what must be said. And if more specifics are required, I propose as a fruitful subject for discussion the implications of the right to neutrality, which is the really important part, and not the right itself. Because every specific right or law, in addition to the primary attributes it has as such, is the strict expression of enormous historical realities, of gigantic and sometimes age-long struggles that have reached a point of equilibrium precisely in that right or law. The precise outline of every particular law—as of every institution—is the profile or frontier of forces in collision that, exhausted with fighting, settled on a compromise. To destroy one law without replacing it with another is to conjure up the infinite capacity that man—who was once a beast—still has for fighting. Let me point out that all this was in part said by me and in part hinted at in a long article published around 1938 in the English maga-

zine *The Nineteenth Century*, with the title "Concerning Pac-
ifism."* What I announced there is happening now and filling
the newspapers. This gives a modicum of authority to what
I have just said.†

*Later included in *The Revolt of the Masses* as part of "Epilogue for English-
men." [Ed.]
†At the end of the manuscript of this lecture, as an indication of the notions
with which it was to end, there are only these abbreviated notes: The
crow's nest. The stupid world. Struggle by proxy. [Ed.]

4

The global nature of the crisis. The end of
Enlightenment. What remains?—A sense of loss.
The similarities of Descartes's and our situation.
Unadorned life. Our paradoxical ignorance of
life. The experience of life. The ambiguity of the
term "life." General theory of human life and
general theory of individual life. Appendix: The
mummy of philosophy.

. . . *

To SAY that the highest courts of appeal— the norms of truth,
morality, law, politics, economy—have failed us is to say
that we don't know what anything is, in other words, what
man and the world *are*, what we *are*; we don't know where
we stand in their regard; we can't count on them—in my
philosophy, "counting on something" is a technical term
denoting an extememly important concept—or, to reduce
both expressions to a third and final one: we have neither a
world beyond us nor a proper "humanity" with us. I don't
think I need remind you that of course pieces, clumps of
both theoretical and practical reason—bits of this science or
that, this *corpus-juris* or another, of some morality, a certain
kind of poetry, or of painting—do remain intact, that is,
remain as the particular fragments they are, and that because
they have never given us cause to doubt them, still seem

---

* The beginning of this lecture is missing. [Ed.]

valuable to us. But since the overall framework that was their ultimate base and to which they belonged—and wherein lay their deepest significance—are reduced to ruins, it avails nothing that they remain intact as fragments of a whole. Obviously areas of logic and elements of mathematics still hold firm; but what good is this if ultimately Logic itself and Mathematics itself are suspect, questionable as to the status of their truth? Something more curious still: all our present laws of physics are much more exact and sure than any previous ones; yet what comfort is this if today we are ignorant of the "laws of physics in general" as applied to the reality to which they supposedly refer?

The world in which man lived thirty years ago is threatened now—notice I only say threatened—by a terrible revolution that may change our world or cosmos into chaos. (At the appropriate time we will analyze in detail the meaning of "world," "cosmos," and "chaos." For the present they retain their usual meanings.) The era that began in the eighteenth century and ended in 1900 has been called the Enlightenment, *Aufklärung*, the Century of Light. Man thought that he had finally managed to see things clearly. But that "light" has now gone out, and again man is surrounded with shadows and darkness. Or, to use another image, he is not on solid ground; he feels he is falling through empty space.

But if we no longer have anything to count on as we did before, what is left that is solid, unquestionable? Is there nothing, amid all the collapse, the going up in smoke, the fading away, that we can stand on, dig our feet into so as to try and recover a sense of clarity and certainty?

We have nothing but this sense of falling through empty space. No one in our social environment can offer any authentic direction or clear guidelines. All that remains is for us to feel "like a solitary person going forward in shadows"; in other words, each is abandoned to his own, individual life, his lived experience of discouragement at this loss.

In history, no real situation, no concrete situation is ever repeated. But in every historical situation there is a certain shell or cluster of factors—its abstract components—that is identical to those in other situations. This will be explained at a future date. At present I just want you to take note of what I say: all that remains to us, the only thing not in doubt, is the feeling of being "like a solitary person going forward in shadows." But these are only metaphors, aren't them? Imaginings, inappropriate in a philosopher, wouldn't you say? Yet listen to this: "But like a solitary person going forward in shadows. . . ." René Descartes wrote that in 1635 or 1636 in the second part of his *Discourse on Method*, which would be published in 1637 and amount to his program— his starting place and preliminary sketch of the foundations of the entire modern era, especially as far as physics and mathematics, the exemplary sciences, were concerned and the pragmatic techniques they made possible. With these words Descartes gave an admirable description of his situation, the situation in which he began and which dictated his means of forward motion or *method*. So that I can use his very same words, the same metaphor—let the ragtail intellectuals gnash their teeth— because, through a particular conjunction of abstract elements, Descartes's situation is identical to our own.

Moreover, as was to be expected, given this abstract identity of situations, the reasoning with which our philosophy begins has the same abstract structure as Descartes's. And so we say:

The whole theoretical and practical interpretation of reality that made up the fabric of our lives— or so we believed— has failed us, but for there to be such a total failure there has to be someone or something it fails. This someone or something that is the object of this failure and, in the light of it, affirms its own unquestionable and infallible reality is "our life," that of each one of us. This is what we are left with, this is what we have, each of us: the act of living.

Recall in briefest summary Descartes's reasoning. When he is forced to doubt everything and, thus, can no longer affirm that anything he once believed in really *exists*, he discovers that for this to be so, for everything to be in doubt and hence *not exist*, at least his doubt must not itself be in doubt, and the doubt and its doubter must exist. This is why he said *dubito, cogito ergo sum* (I doubt, that is, I think, because doubt is a kind of thinking, and I therefore exist). In the course of these lectures we cannot forgo a rigorous, detailed confrontation with this Cartesian proposition or thesis—from which our whole modern era has emerged, the way a whole forest issues from a single seed—but speaking didactically, this is not the appropriate moment to undertake a hand-to-hand struggle with such a formidable teacher. Suffice it to say that our present doubt is even more radical than Descartes's; we doubt that doubt is actually a *cogitatio*, or thought, at all; we doubt the Scholastic, Aristotelian, and, ultimately, Greek notion of existence; and we even doubt the traditional idea of truth or logic. Descartes, unwittingly, and when he thought he was doubting everything, continued to believe in the Scholastic philosophy with which he had meant to make a complete break. Our own situation, therefore, is even more difficult, more precarious than Descartes's, so that we have to go further back than he did, find a broader, more solid, more presuppositionless foundation, which is none other than our very own unadorned life. But just why our life is all this—a broader, more solid, more presuppositionless foundation than any thought or *cogitatio*—will remain unclear unless we begin by seeing with sufficient clarity what "life" is.

We must therefore come to grips as quickly as possible with the strange phenomenon that life is—the life of each one of us.

Although each of our lives is the most elementary and primary thing, something we are always already "in" when we think about anything else, it is a curious fact that philosophy has always turned its back on "life," until the admirable Dilthey discovered it in the last third of the nineteenth century—discovered the obvious, that is.

But if philosophy ignored it, common man, no matter what his station in life, has faced it time and again in the practice of his daily routine. With no theoretical pretentions, out of vital necessity, he had formed ideas about it that were precipitated and crystallized in words, phrases, and idioms of everyday language, even if, through constant use, the latter have lost their expressiveness; like pebbles smoothed in a stream, their meaningful edges have been rounded off, or like newly minted coins worn smooth in passing from hand to hand, they have lost their bright sharpness and await a special discernment, guided by a new intuition of life, to recover their luster and to release their profound meaning once more. Thus our analysis of human life will entail, in part, the rediscovery of the rich and pithy senses of many of our ordinary, colloquial sayings. For these bear the accumulation of the spontaneous "life experience" or vital wisdom that in century after century everyman has unknowingly produced. At another time we shall see that, while astronomy for example is not a part of the stellar bodies it researches and discovers, the peculiar vital wisdom we call "life experience" is an essential part of life itself, constituting one of its principal components or factors. It is this wisdom that makes a second love necessarily different from a first one, because the first love is already there and one carries it rolled up within. So if we resort to the image, universal and ancient as you will see, that portrays life as a road to be traveled or traveled again—hence the expressions "the course of life, *curriculum vitae*, decide on a career"—we could say that in walking along the road of life we keep it with us, know it; that is, the road already traveled curls up

behind us, rolls up like a film. So that when he comes to the
end, man discovers that he carries, stuck there on his back,
the entire roll of the life he led. In other words, he is weighted
down with "life experience," just as the harvest grape in
autumn has hoarded, stored up inside all the summer sun.
This delightful subject, the "life experience," has scarcely
had any attention; until now it has never been raised to the
status of theory. But we shall speak of it repeatedly in these
lectures.

Perhaps we ought to clear up a possible confusion. The
life we have begun to speak of is not biological life. The
totality of organic phenomena that biology calls "life" is
already a theoretical construct produced by man the biolo-
gist as he lives biographically, not biologically, his primary
and fundamental life. Of this life, biology is only one product among others. Biology happens in the biographies of
certain men, the so-called biologists, who thus give their
lives over to the study of organic phenomena, who do this
as an occupation. Of course, in the process they commit the
silly mistake of calling their work biology, which shows they
know very little Greek—in itself nothing to be ashamed of,
although it is shameful that someone without any Greek
should use it and call biological existence, what the Greeks
called zoé, bíos instead. They should call their science zool-
ogy, which would then include botany. Only occasionally
does Aristotle speak of the bíos of animals, but always in
reference to their behavior, never to their organic existence.
The Greek word bíos is life in the sense that interests us,
that is, the biographical sense of conduct and thus in the
predominately biographical sense of human existence—in
the sense in which even the most humble and ignorant man
speaks of his "life" and declares that it is "going well," or
"going badly," "that he has failed or triumphed in life," or
that he is "fed up with life," in the sense that a lover, at least
the Spanish variety, calls his beloved "my life," when he

experiences several of those tropical moments so common in love. For the Greeks this was *bíos*. It is only this silly error of the biologists that keeps us from calling the study we are presently engaged in *biology*, which would have been the best name for it.

My plan in this and the other January lectures is to describe the structure of life, and since life is always "my life," the life of each one of us, I want to help you acquire an intellectual grasp of it or, to put it in an unpedantic way, to have each of you realize with complete clarity the shape and contour of that most precious reality that is the existence of each of us qua life. Each of you lives his life and knows about his life thanks to this "life experience" I referred to a moment ago, which constantly accompanies and intervenes in your life, forming part of it. But this "life experience" or vital learning or what the ancients called "wisdom" is practical knowledge, and not a theoretical pass at defining life and discovering its structure or consistency, its essential anatomy.

Since life is always mine, belonging to the *I* each one of us is supposed to be, the study we must undertake is autobiography. I want to awaken in each of you an unmediated view, direct evidence, of what your own personal life is, so that what I say will be first of all understandable by reference to the immediate intuition you have of your own lives and so that, second, you can weigh what I say, that is, decide for yourselves if what I enumerate and formulate coincides with the very lives you lead.

My task, as you see, is paradoxical and daring; presently, we shall see how it is also inevitably limited as well. It is paradoxical and daring not because I alone am to do your biographies, a thing that seems problematic since I don't know most of you or, more exactly, don't know you that well, but because I am to write your *auto*biographies. Just how this is possible, and if in an absolute sense it is at all possible, is something we shall only learn when our task is done. In fact, in these lectures, I shall have to imagine myself from the place where I am on this side of the table to the place out there where each of you is; I shall have to pierce the fabric of your personal lives and temporarily become a kind of *cambrioleur* of your inner secrets. Even more, I must guide you to arcane regions of your own being where you yourselves rarely visit, force you to descend to the hidden basement of your existences where the tender vessels of the drama that is each of your lives quiver in the dark—lives that because they are so dramatic, you long to evade or disguise with a camouflage of quips, jokes, or, instead, feigned seriousness, business, ambition, scientific work, or else amusements, bridge, golf, café conversation, the gesticulations of political action, singing, or listening to wailing *fados*. We shall see how one part of the consistency or essence of our lives is the continual tendency to disguise or to hide from ourselves, to not want to see one's own authentic reality, to raise a rumpus so as not to hear oneself; in short, to distract oneself from oneself—so much so that a large and energetic portion of one's life is deliberately dedicated to creating distractions. Or, to put it differently, we could say that each of us is mostly busy avoiding being what he inevitably is.

Notice that his dangerous enterprise of violating the secrets of your lives is not the result of some impertinent whim on my part; instead it is the inevitable starting place for a philosophy that really *is* philosophy, as opposed to one that *was* and is no longer. There are two reasons why this is so: one, that as we have just seen, each of us can only count on the plain, unadorned fact of living—everything else is doubtful, questionable, problematic—and this living is an event that happens to each of us exclusively. That is, properly and originally "life" means "my life," the life of the "I" that each of us is. Life is nontransferable: no one, as will become clear, can live my life even to the smallest degree. In the course of living, how I come to find there what I call "the life of others," and just what is meant by this "life of another"—these are things we will attempt to explain later. The other reason a philosophy that is current must start out from autobiography—that is, from the life of each of us—is that such a philosophy must resolve to understand reality as it is, concretely. Whereas the philosophies that once were, even while acknowledging that *being* was concrete specific being, as they had to do, still managed to avoid closing with it on one pretext or another. They were reluctant to base an ontology on the concrete entity and instead substituted it with being in general, a being that in consequence was an abstraction of authentic being. This is particularly clear in Saint Thomas [Aquinas], who translates and paraphrases Aristotle as follows: *Existentia est singularium, scientia est de universalibus.* This is why previous philosophers were vaporous, diffuse, unreal, and utopian.

At first, our new enterprise seems impossible from this point on. For how can I speak of the life of each of you if I only have access to my own life and must perforce start there? Our undertaking is complicated and difficult, but there is a simple observation that will free it of a great deal of its apparent foolhardiness since it promises that I can go on speaking for a long time about each of your lives while, in fact, I am speaking about what I discover in my own life. For we all say "my life," and the identical name renders it likely that, for all they are different in detail of outline, our lives have the same structure or anatomy, which is also what makes the individual differences of our personal destinies possible. This makes a *General Theory of Human Life* possible which, since we can't call it *biology*, we will call *biognosis*. But is this not to backslide in the direction of a philosophy of generalities instead of realities, like all previous philosophies? In our case such a misstep would be especially serious inasmuch as in our terminology "human life" is a basic, formal term meaning "individual life," the absolutely singular life of each of us. Is it not contradictory, then, to write a *General Theory of Individual Life?* This is something to determine as we advance in our project. It would be useless for me to say anything on this point here and now because, until you have a clear view of the shape of that reality that each of your lives is, my words will lack the precision that we require. It is a staggering but undeniable thing: each of you is his life and no more, yet you have never seen that life, never observed it, never taken stock of it or been aware of it. Man lives habitually inmersed in his life, a castaway in it, dragged along moment by moment in the rushing torrent of his destiny; that is to say, he lives like a sleepwalker who is only interrupted by brief flashes of clarity when he glimpses the foreign face of the fact of his life, just as lightning, with its sudden glare, allows us to perceive, in the blinking of an eye, the dark center of the black cloud from which it issues. Calderón was right in a much more concrete and trivial sense than he intended: life *is* a dream, because any reality that is not self-transparent, that does not possess itself fully, that remains locked in itself, that fails to escape and rise above itself, is a dream. In this there is no difference between the uneducated man and the scientist. Even the physicist is a sleepwalker and not just in his daily life but when he does physics as well; he sleepwalks as he creates his science. Physics is a dream, a mathematical dream. The only possibility man has of waking, of coming to his senses and living with perfect clarity is precisely by doing philosophy. In this sense life is inevitably one of two things: either sleep walking or philosophy. I say in all honesty at the outset: philosophy is no dream; philosophy is insomnia—a perpetual qui vive, the desire for an eternal midday clarity and an eager vocation of vigilance and light. In this sense, but only in this sense, Fichte was correct when he said: To philosophize means essentially not to live; to live means essentially not to philosophize. But this would be an admission that life has no other shape than the one it drags about blindly and sleepily.

Let us, without further ado, find the shortest way to a perception of, a direct contact with, life itself, so that it stands before us with its peculiar profile; let us seek the shortest path to a clear and unadorned view of this very thing we refer to when we speak of human life. The trouble is that this shortest path begins with my having to ask you a question I hope you will not find impertinent since I myself am going to try to answer it as best I can.

The question is: Why are you here? I mean why is each of you here now? This is not a joke. The question is far more serious than it appears. Because it is a fact that none of you is just here in the sense that a star at this moment is on a certain point of its orbit, out of blind, mechanical necessity. No, you are here because you came here, because you brought yourselves here, because you wanted to come.*

Addendum to Lecture 4: The Mummy of Philosophy†

Philosophy died a long time ago—although its mummy and its skeleton, for generations past, have been on display at certain regular hours in the Faculties of Philosophy. What was said in these Faculties was more or less clever, exact, pleasant; but, ultimately, it meant nothing to us. Sometimes it was better, sometimes worse; but it didn't stay with us. Now, philosophy, when it really is philosophy, ought to awaken terror, enthusiasm in us, uneasiness, curiosity, exaltation, special delight. This always happens in our lives

---

*The remaining part of this lecture is missing. [Ed.]
†This addendum includes the text of Ortega's handwritten notes that he intended to use in his oral presentation. Apparently he did not have time to include them in his lecture.

in its greatest moments when life becomes expansive, grows, is life and yet more than life. When it is really something special and not merely conventional, not just talk, philosophy simply cannot be the gray and empty thing that occurs in Philosophy Faculties, but something that happens in each one of us, that is each one of us.

But today if anyone could create philosophy, do philosophy in this unique, authentic sense, that is, in concrete terms and without flattery or evasions, if anyone were capable of doing serious philosophy and thereby making people cry and laugh, making audiences tremble, not with his humor or cleverness, but purely and simply and solely by doing philosophy, what would we say of such a person? What would people think? How strange they would feel, how surprised and amused when they saw the mummy, the ridiculous skeleton that was on display in the classrooms but that didn't "stay with us" actually begin to move, look around and see and be seen, and say things, terrible and dramatic, funny things that overwhelmed us, possessed us as each one possesses his own life; that, right from the very beginning, took us violently and painfully, thrillingly by storm, and remained there within—forever—that is, a philosophy that each day when the lecture was over, instead of remaining behind in the classroom—like a stuffed bird in the national history museum—simply "stayed with us."

5

The characteristics of philosophy. Christian intellectualism. Aristotle's presuppositions. Philosophy is the awareness of problems. Logic's impossibility. Six things that follow. The present crisis: A philosophical situation. The case of theoretical reason and of practical reason. The decline of Europe. The targetless arrow. The loss of final courts of appeal.

I SAID that no human activity is comprehensible unless we trace our way back to the situation that gave rise to it. And if this is true to some extent of all activities, it is especially true when the activity is philosophy in the best sense: that strange occupation to which certain men dedicate their lives, abstruse, impalpable, almost acrobatic because of the apparently unjustifiable subtleties and paradoxes that seem mere word games; even a quite useless activity by comparison with the natural sciences and their rich technological yield that is so materially beneficial; in fine, a pretentious activity that is almost proud of its consubstantial uselessness, but one that, nevertheless, or rather for this very reason, considers itself the only, the supreme and authentic wisdom. Both these points were formulated by Aristotle when, in comparing this science with the others, in the early paragraphs of his *Metaphysics* he said: *anankaióteral pásai* (all the other sciences are more necessary, in the sense of more useful) *presbýtate oudemia* (but none is so august). Naturally, at

the proper time we will perform some surgery on this saying of Aristotle's, for while it may be true when taken in a
loose sense, when taken seriously and given a precise meaning it turns out to be a gross error. This is an allusion to the
important fact that the Greeks—who discovered both the
intellect or reason, as well as theory—were so taken with it
that they valued it above all else. The result was that while
reason could demand justification of everything else on its
terms, it was its own justification, needing no other beyond
its own existence and activity. Therefore, this apotheosis—
in the strictest sense of the word—this beatification or dei-
fication by the Greeks of the intellect, or *lógos*, of theory,
which among other things was responsible for the first words
of the Gospel of Saint John: In the beginning was the logos
or reason, and reason existed *a beira de* [along side] God, *kai
theós en o lógos* (and Reason itself was God), this apotheosis
of the intellect, as I said, that together with the rest of the
Hellenic treasure was passed on to European culture—Saint
Thomas was an important link in the chain—is now what
has come to be called "intellectualism." Too often we forget
that beneath its cover of revealed dogma, Western Christianity, European Christianity is intellectualistic and a for-
tiori rationalistic. We only have to remind ourselves that, if
perhaps not the most brilliant man then at least the most
characteristic representative of Catholicism in the last four
hundred years, the great Bossuet, said that even God Himself "had to be right." And the remarkable thing is that De
Bonald, the most reactionary of reactionaries, the super-
reactionary, quotes this saying of Bossuet a century or so
later and subscribes to it with great enthusiasm. This is an
exemplary fact that will stand for countless others as proof
of the prestige of reason in the last third of the seventeenth
century: even God was obliged to be reasonable—something which would have shocked fifteen-century Christians,
who were more or less imbued with Occam's thought, and

which Descartes, two hundred years before Bossuet, would have rejected out of hand. It is true that Bossuet, as I intimated, was far from being a revolutionary and a religious innovator—since he was certainly the most characteristic Catholic that ever existed—also said: "I should like the Church to be flexible always and to move always forward," a position that as everyone knows, or should know, serves to distinguish Catholicism from Protestantism. But my generation, and in a fundamental way I was probably first in this, saw how imperative it was that we rebel against this dogged "intellectualism"; and we decided, for unavoidable reasons that will presently be given, that the intellect too must justify itself to human life, since it is merely a specific, particular function of life—valid only when it is an integral part of the organism of our life. In my short book *The Modern Theme*, containing lectures I delivered in 1921, you will find this stated as the philosophic enterprise that our era must accomplish, as in fact has been the case.

But to return to our main point and to leave aside for now the question of whether or not, as Aristotle held, philosophy is the most august wisdom, since that would oblige us to define "august"—a Latin term that corresponds to the Greek, *presbýtatos*. Such an extremely suggestive theme should be left for a more propitious moment, that is to say when, farther down wind in the course, we have a chance to speak of the state, of authority, of *auctoritas*, and when in asking what *authority* is and especially what the *auctoritas patrum* (the authority of the Roman senate) is—a concept that is no less than the key to and the secret of the whole portentous history of Rome—much to our surprise, we discover that authority, author, augury, and *augustus* all have the same root and contain the same idea. This is why during the Empire, when the senate lost its true *autoritas*, the first emperor or prince, Octavian, was given the title *Augustus*, which would continue to be the name of the supreme imperial magistrate, both in the period of the *principatum* and after Diocletian in the era of the *dominatum* or lordship.

The real truth of Aristotle's sentence lies in its presuppositions, which appear in earlier and later paragraphs, and which it attempts to summarize; that is, that philosophy is fundamental wisdom since it deals with primary and ultimate, or basic, problems, and because its purpose is to treat them in a fundamental way. It is this "fundamentalism" of philosophical thought that distinguishes it from other forms of knowledge, especially from the sciences, which, far from dealing with fundamental problems, only handle problems that, in principle, admit of solution, problems that are already as tame as domestic animals, problems already half-solved, that come under investigation half-drugged, the way trained lions are when they enter the ring. By contrast, the problems of philosophy are absolute problems and are absolutely problems, with no checks on their unexpected behavior. They are fierce problems that cause human existence so much of the anguish and pain it must suffer, with no sign of any solution; for indeed, they have none and perhaps never will. This is why philosophy is the only knowledge that counts as knowledge even without being able to solve its problems. Even if, as a human occupation it is a constant failure, it is still justified since the strength of philosophy, unlike other modes of knowledge—science, technology, experimental knowledge or worldly wisdom, and so forth—lies not in the correctness of its solutions but in the inevitability of its problems.

From this we can see that in one sense philosophy is not a science but something else that may have a higher or lower rank in the hierarchy of knowledge. Never forget that after its initial steps the first time that philosophy achieved self-consciousness was in the exquisite figure of Socrates, who the Italian poet Pascoli describes in prison when he was about to down the eternal poison that in one form or another every authentic intellectual ends up drinking:

E nel carcere in tanto era un camuso
Pan boschereccio, un placido Sileno
di viso arguto e grossi occhi di toro.

Well, this snub-nosed woodland Pan, this placid Silenus
with astute gaze and great bull's eyes—*probably the first man
to invent and use the name, philosophy*—defined his peculiar
activities in the squares and gymnasiums of Athens as the
knowledge that one doesn't know. A strange kind of knowledge indeed, in which what is known, the content, is one's
own ignorance! This strange science was what Cardinal
Cusano—undoubtedly the most brilliant, perhaps the *only*
brilliant figure of the fifteenth century—would call "wise
ignorance" some nineteen hundred years later. Philosophy,
then, is above all an acute consciousness of problems, not a
petulant certainty as to solutions. It is certainly true that
just once in Plato's writings we see Socrates almost dis-
claiming his attitude of wise ignorance or incipient wisdom.
That was on a warm summer day, at noon, when Socrates
led his disciple Phaedrus to the outskirts of the city, and to
a grove of plane trees by the River Kephisos, a place of
shady coolness. At siesta time, the time for abandonment—
that the Greeks called *mesembria*—Socrates told Phaedrus
this secret: "In Athens I say I don't know anything, but that
isn't quite true. There is one matter, one only in which I
am learned and even an expert. That is *ta erotiká*, in matters
of love." While they spoke, above their heads in the plane
trees ancient summer crickets bowed their rough fiddles.

Philosophy has an unwarranted reputation for being difficult. What happens is that since philosophy is such a fundamental activity, there is no way of understanding it unless
the problems that spark or ignite it are kept clearly in mind.
This is why we spoke briefly in the last lecture of the
extremely problematical situation of man today. As regards
both theoretical and practical reason, the principles and
suppositions of Western life have suddenly turned into

questions, enigmas. I referred to the "crisis of the foundations" of the exemplary sciences—physics, mathematics, and
logic—that together until recently constituted what could
most properly be called intellect or reason. Now physics
has been separated from the concept of matter; the principle
of causality has disappeared; the laws of physics have ceased
to be solid causal laws and have become mere statistical ones
that speak only of probabilities; and the physicist admits he
can no longer tell if physics is still knowledge in the usual
sense of the word—this amounts to a confession that he
doesn't know what he is doing now when he does physics.
It isn't necessary for you to understand all these points. The
time will come when all is sufficiently clear. What you must
do is absorb the following simple fact: this is how contemporary physicists think of physics; and the same is true of
mathematicians and logicians, even though logic is the prototype of the purest science and most authentic theory, the
touchstone, yardstick, and judge of all the rest.

Today it would be a good idea to dot our "i's" and cross
our "t's". When I remark that logic, in its recent attempt to
provide itself with a sound and completely rigorous foundation—that is, to actualize itself and cease to be merely a
program and a project as it has been until now—discovered
that this was quite impossible, that the underpinnings of
logic were not logical but illogical assumptions, and, therefore, that logic was in large measure and, so to say, *consub-
stantially* illogical, and that in consequence *there is no logic*, I
expect you to understand exactly what I say.

Ladies and gentlemen, I am speaking with a certain rigor,
and until now *logic* has meant something very precise: this
was the name of our most exact rational theory, in which
nothing was vague or *ad libitum*, in which everything was
either self-evident and therefore proven—as seemed the case
with its first principles—or was susceptible of exact proof,
as was believed to be the case with everything that was
deducible from those principles. The truth of logical theory

was not just another truth; it was absolutely founded on reason, absolutely proven. But when *that* logic achieved its most exact, perfect, and inclusive shape—in studies carried out in the last fifty years—the result of this very exactness, perfection, and all-inclusiveness was the discovery that *that* logic, what the word had referred to for the last twenty-five hundred years, was impossible. Therefore:

1. The catastrophe in logic—keep this clearly in mind—did not derive from any flaw in the thought traditionally known as logic but, on the contrary, from its extraordinary fine-tuning in recent years.

2. Since throughout the history of philosophy logic has been synonymous with the general notion of truth—to such an extent that the most brilliant logician of all time, the giant, the all-but-superhuman Leibniz called his logic the *doctrina veritatis in universum* (the theory of general truth)—this catastrophe in logic means that the traditional notion of truth is in jeopardy.

3. It is literally and strictly speaking correct to say *there is no logic*, since what used to be logic now turns out to be illogical. Not merely have certain of its principles been proven false—as I said to make things simpler—rather the entire corpus of logic began to reveal its illogicality, and it became clear that concepts were never such that they could be handled logically since, strictly speaking, they were mere approximations. Or, to give another example, if we open what I consider the most recent important book on mathematical logic— logic's most esoteric branch—by the American William Van Orman Quine, called *Mathematical Logic* (New York, Norton, 1940)—my own English-language publisher, by the way—we read that "there must always be indemonstrable mathematical truths." But indemonstrable truths are clearly not logical ones. And just what this other class of "truth" may be that is true without being logical, no one seems to know.

4. Logic, held by the best minds of Greece, Rome, and

Europe to be the one this-worldly thing that was absolutely not an illusion but real and altogether dependable, has been unmasked and shown to be just another illusion that man had nurtured and must now relinquish: a utopia, something merely imaginary, a *desideratum*, an ideal we believed was safe and secure—since logic was invented in 480 B.C.—for the last twenty-five hundred years. What a tenacious illusion! What we wouldn't give to have another illusion with the power to hold us in thrall for the next twenty-five hundred years!

5. It isn't that traditional logic is no longer taught in high school and universities. The logic that has lost its value as exemplary and absolute *truth* continues to be useful, albeit downgraded to approximate and practical truth. Yet notice how the most contradictory thing about our traditional notion of logical truth is that in the end it turned out to be no more than a practical truth, useful for minor and approximate subjects. This is what happened with traditional (Euclidean) geometry, which now is still useful for short distances but inapplicable when a geometry of great distances is called for—what Einstein designated as a *Ferngeometrie* [long-distance geometry].

6. To find out that logical thought is utopian is also to raise the possibility that a different kind of thought may exist that is not utopian, or much less so—a new thought we could still designate as *logical*, provided the term were understood in a new sense. And this future thought, at whose creation certain of us have been working, will be, or so we intend, more precise than the old logical thought, that is, more adequate to what it attempts to think and, at the same time, less logical than traditional logic, or not logical at all.

7. The present juncture is a specifically philosophical situation, which means that it is characterized in one of two ways: either we are in a situation where, because the visionary way to truth has failed and for the first time, as in ancient Greece, we come up with the intellectual or rational method,

which is just another name for philosophy itself; or our situation is one where, because reason has failed, as has indeed happened, a new method must be found that is neither the rational one of the philosophical tradition nor the visionary one which philosophy replaced; in other words, a new *reason* must be discovered. The latter alternative is the one I believe to be the case. At any rate the new thought that is achieved will result from going beyond the rational method that was used heretofore and is now in crisis; a reason that has failed can only be surpassed by employing means that include it, in other words, rational, philosophical means.

I meant to expand on this point—although given its extension I have said comparatively little—and to explain the recent catastrophe in logic so you would see from this example what the present situation of the intellect or reason amounts to in theoretical terms, and how an awareness of the problematic abyss that has opened for scientists—the feeling that they are suddenly no longer on firm ground but adrift in a labile, insecure element, a sea of doubt—automatically forces them to swim so as to stay afloat and reach dry land and a new shore. Instead of logic we could have spoken in similar terms about mathematics and physics, but they would have taken up too much of our lectures. My purpose was not to study the new methodology required by the particular sciences, but to lay down principles on which the new methodology could be based, in short, to develop a philosophy that, since it must deal with problems more fundamental than those of any previous philosophy, must itself be more radical than any previous philosophy. This should enable you to put a precise meaning to the sentence that begins the paragraph I read you from Husserl, and that said: "The present condition of European sciences necessitates radical investigations of sense." These radical investigations are that more radical philosophy we have been working to achieve.

But it may have occurred to you that the catastrophe which

overtook the foundations of theoretical reason and the exemplary sciences, while still a catastrophe, has a positive valence as well: first, in that it originated not in any failure of the intellect but, on the contrary, resulted from its greater perfection and refinement; and second, because when it is authentic, the intellect is always a positive force, whether it sets out to be so or not—as is clear once we realize that while the discovery of an error seems at first glance an entirely negative event, on further consideration it is also, *ipso facto*, the discovery of a new truth. You would naturally think that the discovery that something was false would be like a light going out; nevertheless, it has just the opposite effect: a new and brighter illumination. This inevitable, positive valence is what characterizes authentic intellect, just as a negative one characterizes the pseudo-intellect. This is the source of that fatal negativity that all village pseudo-intellectuals exude when they write or speak—the inner nothingness they are made of.

For all the above reasons, the other day I was able to diagnose the present attitude of man as regards the crisis of reason in a way that, put a little differently today, would go as follows: man is ambivalent about his reason; he still believes in it but now he believes it has limits as well.

The situation is different in the sphere of practical reason, which we exemplified by alluding to the disappearance of moral reason and to the complete collapse of law, an element that seemed absolutely necessary as a recourse and standard for life in human society. Even here, nevertheless, the catastrophe has a positive side because if, as I said, for the first time in history all established rights and institutions have ceased to function without any others having appeared to replace them, this is partly due—*but only in part*—to the fact that Western experience is already too rich in questions of law. For example, in fourteen hundred years so many forms of government have been tried and proved inherently

defective that it is difficult to discover a form that is new
and different from past ones and that can still sway us. This
accumulation of so many life-experiences is one of the
inconveniences of advanced maturity. On reaching maturity the peculiar human "state" we call "having illusions"
becomes more difficult to achieve. The truth is that, whether
we want to be or not, in matters of governance we Europeans are in the "once bitten, twice shy" category.*

Unfortunately, however, practical reason—morality, law,
government, customs, and so forth—unlike theoretical reason, cannot exist in isolation but needs must engage mankind's passion and blindspots, the economic structure of
society, the poverty or wealth of each nation, and the pressure some nations exert upon others. And all of these elements are especially unfavorable today for Europeans and
their rational culture. Herein lies the extreme gravity of the
situation. But this is not my subject. However, it would be
inexcusable not to say at least this: twenty years ago I showed
at some length that Europe would soon reach the point where
it would lose what control over the world it had exercised
for the last four hundred years—unless it immediately discovered a drastic remedy—and that this loss of command,
which would cause Europeans to lose self-confidence and
faith in their historic role, risked making them mean and
vicious, causing them to become completely demoralized;
then they would be inert reactors instead of agents of his-

*Let me make clear that the allusion to certain types of regimes—I have
no qualms about repeating it, they do not represent political right at all but
are rather emergency surgery, orthopedics—is not made with reference to
any country, since it refers to a greater or lesser degree to all regimes. This
audience should not seek political allusions, what are known as "political"
ones, in anything I say here, for I know very well—and shall demonstrate
in due time—what politics is; in fact, in spite of what people here still
believe, it has now begun to irritate and disgust other Europeans to the
point where the really serious loser in the civil and governmental battles of
recent years will be precisely that politics that has senselessly tried to invade,
overrun, and asphixiate every area of our lives. [Ortega. Insertion by Ed.]

tory, perhaps even slaves of the other continents; in short, they would repeat the ineluctable destiny of all people who once ruled and then ceased to rule, and who were then condemned to obey and only obey—the definition of a slave—becoming a nation of *fellahs*. *Fellah* is the Egyptian laborer—residue of the first and thrice-thousand-year-old Empire that ceased to make history twenty-five hundred years ago—who, reduced to a vegetable or botanical existence, now plows the selfsame furrow every day, head bowed ingloriously over his plow; while, taking no notice of them, the marvellous and ever distinct event we call historical life, the march of history, goes on around them. This is not the place to say whether or not this has already happened to Europe: I can only say that in view of events today I feel a certain chill and an uneasiness because of my prophecy.

Of course, if you prefer, we can take things less tragically and, feigning a romantic consolation, wallow with morbid narcissism in our degeneracy and say—with convincing panache—as our Andalusian poet Manuel Machado does, that:

I am much like the peoples who traveled to my land,
My race is the Moorish one, old friend of the sun,
Which first won everything and then lost everything.
Mine is the spikenard soul of Spanish Araby.

Fair enough. That is one kind of consolation; but others are to be preferred.

In every order of life, then, contemporary—not only European—man feels lost, and this awareness of fundamental disorientation must be kept in the foreground. We must not be so cowardly as to shut our eyes to it, for only this desperate sense of being lost can provoke a healthy, saving reaction in us. Later we will see why everything of value that we have accomplished was due to a feeling of radical disorientation; and the reverse, that all our misfortunes and disasters came about because one day we felt much too safe.

For mankind, being disoriented—*dépaysé*—is being radically lost: what Husserl expressed by saying that the world has become a problem for us. And this is so because, as we shall soon see—today even, if there is time—man has no choice but to always be doing something in order to live or survive; I almost said he has no choice but to be always doing something on pain of death, but that falls short of the mark since, if he gives up, does nothing and lets himself die, he still does one of the most terrible things he can do—and that is to commit suicide. Thus he always has to do something; but in order to be thus active he must choose an activity, and this choice must be made according to how the world is, how he is, and his life is—so that he can find motives that inspire and justify the choice in his own eyes.

Man, a pure and continual do-ing, a constant activity, is total movement, drawn forward toward a goal. And, for very special reasons we will take up one day, the entity *man*, whose sole reality consists in moving toward a target, is now suddenly without one; nevertheless he must still move forward. To what end? Where does one go when one doesn't have a place in mind? In what direction do the lost turn? For the last thirty years we have had a radical sense of being lost.

In Buenos Aires, shortly before embarking for Lisbon—it will soon be three years ago—the handsomely bound typescript of a course I had given in the Faculty of Philosophy in 1916 was presented to me. Back than I was a young whippersnapper who obviously knew even less than I do now; but I was surprised on reading those old words to see that I had dealt, albeit inadequately, with the great subjects that occupy philosophy today, but back then it had yet to touch on. Among others, already set squarely at the center of philosophy, was the problem of man that Scheler dealt with years later, but without making him the center of philosophy, which is the important thing. Now, in my efforts to explain the enigma that man is I stumbled, way back then, on an image that I, and all philosophy characteristic of our time, could today easily subscribe to. I defined man metaphorically, saying that he possesses the dynamic soul of an arrow that in mid-flight has forgotten where its target lies. Imagine the poor shaft of the arrow vibrating with the inevitable velocity of its flight yet suspended in space, having to move ever forward, without knowing the direction, possessed only of its forward inertia and its sense of loss. Everything around us can be explained as forms of not knowing what to do. Sometimes these forms adopt strange disguises, for some people tend to a frenzied activity or drug themselves with an inauthentic hyperactivity to replace the emptiness of not knowing what to do; and, at the other extreme, there are those who cleave to complete inactivity, quietism, passivity in the face of whatever may occur.

No one knows what to do in politics, as we saw, but, then, neither does the physicist know what he is doing in physics, nor the mathematician in mathematics, nor the logician in logic—to which, given more time, we could have added—nor the poet in poetry, nor the musician in music, the painter in painting, the capitalist with his capital, nor the worker at his work, nor the father with his family, and since the family too is in crisis the relationship between the sexes is also a problem now. Each of these phrases represents a subject about which there is a great deal to say if only Time the Tyrant would allow us so much as a glimpse at it.

Without final courts of appeal there is no direction, and we have lost all final courts of appeal that might have served to direct our lives. Of course the believer has his religion, but religion only directs life—remember this—in the direction of the afterlife. This is why religion neither knows nor presumes to know what political institutions or what modes of thought or what philosophy of economics or what painting style we should choose.

Those of you who are younger will see in times to come if man can in fact live with no thought to whether or not there are final courts of appeal in his life. I shall not live to see it or, at least, to see the situation fully developed, because I have reached that point on the road of existence where one can see, in the distance, closing off the horizon, the rising foothills covered with a fine line of snow that announces the end of the traveler's life.

On all accounts Western man finds himself in an extreme situation, and philosophy is precisely the intellectual reaction to extreme situations. For this reason, if I were asked what exactly the subject of this course has been and will be, I might answer that it has been and will be certainly what goes on in the laboratories of the physicists, in the cogitations of the logicians and mathematicians, but also that it is about what is happening outside this hall, in the streets and squares, the houses and the social clubs, in bars and taverns, in public gatherings and in the secret meetings of government, in the solitude of the worried man and in the exaltation of the crowded masses, on the sea, on earth, in the air and beneath the sea, in the abyss, or even beyond the air, in the stratosphere. It's about all that; that's what it's about!*

*The development of the many themes announced here never took place because the course was interrupted at this point, making this fifth lecture the last one. [Ed.]

Appendices

1: Theology and Philosophy

GOETHE SAID that unlike the animals, man is never only a successor but an inheritor as well. This is certainly correct. At his birth man always confronts forms of life— modes of speech and thought, feeling, construction, private and public conduct, and so forth—that he has to assimilate unless, of course, he is to create them all anew, that is, unless he means to return to the first moment of humanity and be the first man all over again. This first man inherited nothing, which, in a literal sense, is why he is an imaginary creature who never existed. The first man of flesh and blood would have been indistinguishable from the last orangutan. It is by no means clear how a million years ago—I mentioned before the recent calculations that permit us to give this approximate date for the appearance of the species *Homo sapiens* on earth—a creature appeared in nature that was already *human*, or at least humanoid, as the anthropologists say, and no longer a mere anthropoid. About this point I have certain notions that I will not hesitate to divulge at the proper time, that is, at the end of this course, even though they are no more than suspicions.

Those who are fervent believers in Christianity need not be startled by statements such as the above, that is, by talk that we are indistinguishable from the last orangutan or—it comes to the same thing—from the most advanced anthropoid. Neither this nor anything else I say in this course will erode anyone's faith in any way. This is true of not only my philosophical thought, for it would be correct to say that for the last fifty years *no* philosophy, certainly none of the better-known ones, has collided with religious faith. This

213

is not because of any deliberate tactic of evasion but because philosophy has finally seen clearly that it does not speak of the same things as theology. Theo-logy, or *theo-léguein*, is to speak of God and from God, which means, from the perspective of the divine word—which is revelation, *apokalypsis*, and therefore all its concepts are conceived and understood in terms of that word. Whereas philosophy speaks of what is and what is not, according to criteria of human reason and hence is the very opposite of apocalypse: it is theory and therefore intuition and evidence. In this way, and to take an extreme example, what we said before was a reference to the "nature" of man. But the expression "the nature of man" means something quite different in theology and in philosophy. Theologians, too, speak of the *status naturae humanae*—the state or status of man's nature. But here "man's nature" is not the consistency or essence of man as our reason conceives it, which is to say the reality of man in itself and according to the data that it manifests or by which it allows us to grasp it, but instead, understood theologically, the term "man's nature" refers in a formal way to the relation, importance, or relevance of that nature, whatever it may be, to the possibility of salvation. Christianity is a doctrine of salvation and not a theory about problems the way philosophy is. In religion proper there are no problems because its purpose is to be all, and only, solutions. Theory, on the other hand, is first and foremost the awareness of problems, the mind's collision with them, their handling and their uses. Moreover, when theory is most itself, as happens in philosophy, it doesn't need to find solutions in order to be itself, it only has to remain acutely conscious of the unavoidable problems. The strength of philosophy, as distinct from other forms of knowledge—the individual sciences, for example—lies not in the correctness of its solutions but in the inevitability of its problems.

Theology as such has no means to decide the nature of

man, which is why it only defines what it calls the *status naturae humanae*, wherein man's nature already includes the supernatural grace man needs for salvation as well as the preternatural grace he enjoyed before he sinned. A good indication of just how distant the theological idea of *natura humana* would be from philosophy is that for theologians physical immortality, a *donum superadditum praeternaturale*, is part of this *natura humana integra*. Now, as we will see, the most important constitutive characteristic of man is his inescapable, physical death. The first man, Adam, who according to doctrine was immortal before he sinned, is obviously a very different character from the first man who was so much like an orangutan—for the latter was certainly mortal.

2: Faith in Reason

THESE PHILOSOPHY lessons were interrupted unexpectedly by my illness. Thus we have not only lost two whole months but, even worse, most of the momentum of the first five lessons. I gave those lectures over to the accumulation of certain concepts that would convey to you vividly the situation that faces philosophy today, one that because of its precise complexion demands of philosophy a certain reaction, that is, requires that it *be* a certain philosophy and no other. It would not be a good idea to betray our destiny and attempt to change it by spending an equal amount of time repeating what has already been said. Especially since that was but a summary of all I ought to have said, it would make little sense to repeat it. This leaves the alternative of moving forward, taking up our discussion where we left off, while at the same time, and to the extent this is possible, I shall make passing references to what was said earlier, or new remarks concerning it, so as to refresh our memory about the ground already covered.

We said it was characteristic of man's situation today that, always forced to do something to subsist, to carry out activities that are a satisfactory reaction to the difficulties of which life more or less always consists, he presently finds himself without any final court of appeal to direct his conduct. There is nothing within him to appeal to, in the form of firm beliefs, nor anything external such as social norms. This is why he vacilates between the two extremes of inertia or quietism, and a hyperactivity that protects him from a consciousness of his own deep dissatisfaction.

As we observed in the previous lessons all these final courts of appeal—in the theoretical and the practical realms—could be reduced to one: faith in reason as mankind's universal instrument for solving his problems. This reason we defined as the capacity to think things truly, that is, to know their being. Thus the idea of reason includes the themes of truth, knowledge, and being. But it was precisely the incomparable perfection of what had been achieved with the help of the exemplary sciences—logic, mathematics, physics—representing reason at its purest and best, that uncovered grave problems regarding its fundamental principles, problems that reason could not solve since they involved the foundations of that selfsame reason. This means that what is now open to question and to being a problem is not merely a theory or an argument, but reason itself *qua* reason. Yet this automatically puts in question the fundamental themes of truth, knowledge, and being as well. And we suddenly realize, much to our surprise, that these themes had never really been studied correctly and in depth before. This was because they had never before been authentic and dramatic problems; which is indirect proof that ordinary hedonistic curiosity can never guarantee the satisfactory study of an enigma—the enigma must first become an authentic, vital problem for man.

This entire crisis of final courts of appeal can be viewed as the crisis of faith in reason. Previously, when the reigning principles, theories, and norms by which Western man lived lost their hold on individuals and peoples—because they were found wanting, wrong, and therefore illusory—Europe would pass through a period of anxiety and discouragement, of turbulence and scatteredness, which made it behave like an army in defeat. Soon, however, Europeans would recover and do what—according to Machiavelli every defeated army does when it is about to fall apart, that is: *ritornare al segno*, rally around the flag that is always in full view because of its height. And reason was the flag of European community life, the faculty, instrument, or power that had served as arbiter in the orientation of its existence, that directed its action and resolved or reduced its conflicts. But now for the first time in the history of civilization, when mankind was caught at a dangerous juncture and all eyes turned to the familiar standard, it was no longer there, waving on the horizon, or at least not as before.

It disturbs me that the impossibility of giving adequate treatment to such a serious subject forces us to deal with these subtle matters in terms that distort the exact nature of the situation. This is why I made clear in past lectures that any diagnosis would be entirely wrong if it confused the unquestionable diminution of our faith in reason with the suspicion that an alternative faith possessed us, in other words, that we were convinced that the exercise of reason was useless, sterile. Certainly today our notion of reason is vague and confused, but if we sincerely attempt to throw off its discipline, turn our backs on it, and each proclaim, to himself and to others, his right to irrationality, we soon notice that, in one guise or another, rational behavior still speaks to us from the depths of consciousness with its imperative voice, as if to say we have no choice in the matter when it comes *to being rational*. What I have just said—that reason or rationality is one of man's inexorable imperatives, a cry or a voice that resounds deep within him with the commandment: "You must be rational"—contradicts the naive idea, fostered by almost all previous philosophers and now an ingrained tradition, that man is rational: in short, that he possesses a particular quality that constitutes his nature and is called reason. If this were the case, it would be hard to explain why man does not always behave in a rational manner with the same regularity that a stone falls toward the earth's center, the spider spins its web, and the tiger springs at the flank of a passing antelope. But even taking each man at his most rational, we can see that some are more rational than others, and that therefore reason is not a precise quality but has a variable magnitude, so that it is impossible to state a maximum for reason that would represent a standard of total and complete reason. In the past there have been repeated attempts to have reason consist in certain exclusive and determinate characteristics. But always this closed and limited idea of reason was found to be irrational, and new forms of reason, often just the opposite of the time-honored ones, came forth, overwhelming and surpassing the old form of reason. Recall, for example, that the bulk of contemporary mathematics works with numbers and relationships that the Greeks first called "irrational."

This one example will suffice—since it is exceptional and extreme—to show that in fact earlier philosophers left untouched such themes as these.

All modern scientific culture thus far has ultimately been

based on the foundations established by Descartes for the basic disciplines. The solidity of his work, which has managed to resist the wear and tear of three hundred years and is only now in jeopardy, is due to the radical nature of his method.*

3: The Dawn of Historical Reason

AROUND 1860, Dilthey, the greatest thinker of the second half of the nineteenth century, discovered a new reality: human life. It is unusually comic that a reality so important and in such close proximity to man took so long to be discovered and was then simply discovered at a certain time on a certain day, like the phonograph or the formula for aspirin. Still, that is the way it happened and nothing can be done about it. The tapestry of history that seems so full of tragedy when viewed from the front has countless comic scenes woven into its reverse side. In truth, tragedy and comedy are the twin masks of history—its mass appeal.

This strange reality—human life—is neither a physical nor a mental thing. It is not a thing in any sense, nor is it the mode, act, or state of any thing. It is a pure happening, of dramatic character. It is what happens to me and what happens to you where you and I are no more than what is happening to us.

*The manuscript ends here. Probably the subject for the rest of this lecture was the one dealt with in Lecture III of the Buenos Aires cycle, included in this volume under the heading "The six prior theses that Descartes." [Ed.]

The outstanding characteristic of this reality that is mere event is that it possesses a structure in and of itself. Neither physical nor mental reality are given us in structured form; quite the reverse; they are the stuff of reality in search of a structure. Concerned, our minds respond to this defect and give physical and mental phenomena the architecture they lack. Thus physics and psychology are constructions.

On the other hand, nothing in our lives happens to us in isolation, without entailments. Something happens to us *because*, or *in view*, *of* some other thing that happened to us, and, ultimately, because we happen to want to live. If this were not the case and we really didn't want to live, nothing would happen; we wouldn't even have toothaches.

The structure of life, then, is individual, concrete, peculiar to each life. But, at the same time, there is a formal structure to it that makes possible general statements like the following: in living, man always *inhabits* a certain belief about his surroundings and himself. Or, to put it another way: we always live *from within* certain beliefs. Rather than inhabiting earth, man *inhabits* his beliefs. These support each other, because they too have a structure—thanks to which we can speak of fundamental beliefs, a solid ground on which other beliefs rest. This is why the greatest change a human life can undergo is a change in its fundamental beliefs.

Until 1450, Europeans inhabited the belief that there was a supreme being—infinitely powerful and infinitely good— who generously provided them with everything necessary for the conduct of life, including the very meaning of that life. But by the end of the fourteenth century, doubt had already begun to grow within this belief. *Being in* doubt is a way of inhabiting belief as well. During the two centuries of the Renaissance, people inhabited this doubt. With the old belief gone and no new one at hand, through an act of will man feigned belief, pretended to believe. The desire to believe is commensurate with the loss of belief. Epochs of crisis are a time for "resolution," for will power. For this reason the characteristic ensign of the Renaissance was *Vivere risolutamente.*

However, belief is just the oposite of will. It is believing something in spite of ourselves and even against our wishes. With belief man has a feeling of stepping out of himself and into reality.

Shortly after 1600, man left his Renaissance belief behind and took up residence in a new one—the "modern" belief that until a few years ago was the basis of European life. For faith in God modern man substituted faith in reason. The latter was just as much a faith as was the former. Previously it was God who revealed to man what was necessary for the fulfillment of his destiny. Now we believe that if we can make it function properly, the human intellect is the marvelous instrument that will reveal the being of things to us. Although the term "reason" has become less and less precise, we should not forget that its importance lies not in some particular technical quality of the intellect as such but in its function, its use, which is to transcend itself and place very reality before us; suddenly our ideas cease to be merely that, and by means of them the being of things appears, *is revealed.* That is what reason does.

The extraordinary harvest reaped by this new faith was physicochemical science: its many applications transformed man's material life. No belief ever kept its initial promises so well. We must acknowledge that the reason of Galileo and Descartes achieved results that in certain areas surpassed the hopes it had inspired and that in a sense it even outstripped man's most dearly cherished fantasies. No wonder that scarcely thirty years ago reason was still the final court of appeal for Europe, its supreme norm, and a species of this-worldly God.

Nevertheless, now the situation has clearly changed. In what way? To how great an extent? In what direction? It is difficult to say, since I have to weigh my words carefully. With this understood, if I were pressed I would say the situation is now the following: reason's admirable and increasingly successful conquests in certain areas have brought us to a point where we cannot stop believing in reason, and yet, at the same time, reason is no longer *the* belief inhabited by European man.

What is the explanation for this ambivalence? To put it simply: reason promised to solve all man's problems. Re-read *Discourse on Method*, the bible of the new faith. While it solved the problems posed by material objects better than anyone expected, it repeatedly failed in its treatment of strictly human problems. This has made us realize that our famous reason was not the whole of reason but only a physical or naturalistic reason.

This is a limitation to which reason was unnecessarily condemned from the start—although the causes of this mistake are not hard to discover. Under the influence of Greece, reason began as the search for the being of things, where "being" meant something fixed or static, the being that each thing already was. The prototypes for this being were concepts and mathematical entities, with their invariable being, always the same. Since reason recognized that material things were subject to change, it had to find something unchanging amidst the change, something that remained itself. It called this something the "nature" of a thing. And, in fact, what the physical, chemical, and biological sciences seek in phenomena is permanent being, their "nature." Hence the failure.

Now, having lost our complete faith in *that* reason, since Dilthey's discovery we have been free to search for man's "being" without the prejudice of naturalism and Eleaticism. It was suddenly realized that the reason of physics was bound to fail with human problems. *Because man has no "nature,"* no fixed or static, prior or given, nature. Not only does he change as do material things, that is, with that pseudo-change that works within fixed limits according to its own laws; man also changes in a much more important, unlimited way. To speak of man's being, we need a non-Eleatic concept of being, as happened with reference to non-Euclidean space. Man has been Paleolithic man but also the Marquise de Pompadour, Genghis Khan, and Stephan George, Pericles and Charlie Chaplin. Countless ways of being have been adopted by man without his subscribing permanently to any of them.

Each of these ways of being represents a fundamental experience undertaken by man, an experience that once assumed turns out to have limitations. These limitations help him see other ways of being not yet tried. In other words, he becomes one thing *because* before he was something else. Man, who *is nothing*, continually *recreates* himself through the dialectical series of his experiences. Therefore, we can only know what man has been, what he can never be again. The past limits the future. This is why, correctly understood, the science of the past is also the only possible science of the future—in the particular sense in which such a science is possible.

In short, *man has no nature but, instead, a history.*

The time has come for reason—the reason of physics—to throw off this limitation and for man to believe in historical reason. Thus far our reason has not been historical, nor has our history been rational. Or don't you think that if we compressed the ten thousand years of our past we could extract a few drops of a very new and saving reason, of historical reason?

Man needs a new revelation, and this can only come from historical reason.

In spite of appearances, I say it is imminent.

17/11